Wholeness After Betrayal

Restoring Trust in the Wake of Misconduct

ROBIN HAMMEAL-URBAN

Morehouse Publishing
NEW YORK

Unless otherwise noted, the Scripture quotations contained herein are from the New Revised Standard Version Bible, copyright © 1989 by the Division of Christian Education of the National Council of Churches of Christ in the U.S.A. Used by permission. All rights reserved.

This book is intended as general guidance and is not legal advice. If you need more details on your rights or legal advice, contact a legal professional. This book is merely intended as a process for engaging a congregation in healing following misconduct related to a faith community. We accept no liability for any loss or damage whatsoever arising as a consequence of any use of or the inability to use any information contained in this book and you agree to indemnify and hold Church Publishing Incorporated and the author harmless for your use of the information contained in this book. Individuals and congregations are strongly urged to be in contact with their bishop, judicatory chancellor, or parish attorney in addressing actual issues of misconduct. Many of the stories contained herein are true, with names and locations removed to maintain the anonymity of all parties involved.

Morehouse Publishing, 19 East 34th Street, New York, NY 10016

Morehouse Publishing is an imprint of Church Publishing Incorporated.
www.churchpublishing.org

Cover design by Laurie Klein Westhafer
Typeset by Rose Design

Library of Congress Cataloging-in-Publication Data

Hammeal-Urban, Robin.
Wholeness after betrayal : restoring trust in the wake of misconduct / Robin Hammeal-Urban.
    pages cm
Includes bibliographical references and index.
 ISBN 978-0-8192-3177-2 (pbk.)—ISBN 978-0-8192-3178-9 (ebook) 1. Episcopal Church—Clergy—Conduct of life. 2. Episcopal Church—Clergy—Sexual behavior. 3. Sexual misconduct by clergy. 4. Clergy—Sexual behavior. I. Title.
 BX5965.H28 2015
 283'.73—dc23
                            2015001011

Printed in the United States of America

For all courageous victims, congregations, and offenders
who have been transformed by the power of the Holy Spirit
and Grace of God in the aftermath of misconduct.

CONTENTS

ACKNOWLEDGMENTS

So much gratitude, so little space on a page.

I am profoundly grateful to the Rt. Rev. Andrew "Drew" D. Smith (retired Bishop Diocesan of Connecticut), for hiring me in 2000. Together, by trial and error, Drew and I figured out ways to support congregations and restore trust after misconduct. Much of this book reflects the concepts that Drew and I co-created and refined over the years. Our work was not done in isolation but with gifted colleagues, including all those who served on our diocesan Pastoral Response Policy Advisory Group. Many thanks to the Rt. Rev. Ian T. Douglas, for allowing me to continue this work and take time to write this book.

I'm also grateful for all those who, decades ago, began working to bring to light misconduct in the Episcopal Church, when many refused to see or speak of it; and for each victim, complainant, offender, and congregation that I have had the privilege to work with. I have been honored to be with each of you in the midst of crisis and possibility of new life.

I'm grateful for my companions along the way including all who served on the Province I Executives & Canons Group, Title IV Working Group and Safe Church Network. Your knowledge, presence, and encouragement sustained me while working amidst some deeply broken relationships in our Church.

I'm grateful to the Rev. Sarah Shofstall and an unnamed courageous victim/complainant who read this manuscript. Both provided wise and valuable insight.

I'm grateful for Sharon Ely Pearson, my friend and editor, for her expertise and time spent fine-tuning this manuscript, but particularly for her steadfastness in shepherding this project over a span of five years.

I'm grateful for my friends who still seem to love me, even though they don't hear from me for weeks at a time; my current colleagues who encourage me, hold me in prayer, and are gracious even when I am tired and cranky; my parents who have been exuberant supporters throughout this project; and my children, now young adults, Colin and Kelsey, for their encouragement and understanding of why I was not always home when they were younger.

And finally, I'm grateful for my husband, Ralph. This book has been a long haul for you, too, and there is much to thank you for: for sharing your writing and proofreading expertise with me, and for your encouragement and support for over thirty years, particularly this past year. I'm not at all sure I could have done this without you by my side.

FOREWORD

◇◇◇

Robin Hammeal-Urban gets right to the heart of the matter in the opening pages of chapter 1: "At its core, congregational misconduct is a betrayal of trust by a leader who puts his or her needs before those of the people to whom he or she ministers. In essence, the leader abuses the power bestowed by virtue of holding a position of leadership in a church."[1] Putting one's own needs before the needs of those over whom one has power results in a disordered relationship—one distorted to the point where wholeness and trust give way to hurt and betrayal. The misappropriation of power for one's own ends is rightly understood as abuse. For Christians the misappropriation of power is seen as a manifestation of our human sinfulness.

In the Catechism of the Book of Common Prayer of The Episcopal Church the question is asked: What is sin? The answer given is: "Sin is the seeking of our own will instead of the will of God thus distorting our relationship with God, with other people, and will all creation."[2] In our sinfulness we turn our backs on God, we deny God's image in others and ourselves, and we destroy the goodness of God's handiwork in the world. In our sinfulness, God-given right-relation gives way to alienation, separation, and abusive power-over relationships. Such disorder is not of God; is not God's intention for creation.

Thanks be to God we are not left alone in our sinfulness. Holy Scripture is the story of God's love and desire to effect right-relation no matter how much we distort our relationships with God, other people, and creation. The opening acts of Genesis tell us that God

---

1. Hammeal-Urban, 10.

2. "An Outline of the Faith," in The Episcopal Church, *The Book of Common Prayer* (New York: The Church Hymnal Corporation, 1979), 848.

brought all things into being through a process of differentiation: light from darkness, the heavens from the waters, earth from the seas, plants and vegetation from the land, creatures from waters and the earth, and then humanity, male and female. "And God saw that it was good." God-given differences are the building blocks of positive, life-giving relationships. In our differences we are given the gift of right-relation.

But these differences, particularly differences in power can easily be corrupted and misused. As the story goes on, no sooner had God created humanity than we turned our backs on God and one another, desiring to live unto ourselves and our own devices and desires. The seeking our own will instead of the will of God results in disordered, distorted relationships between us and God, us and other people, us and all creation.

These disordered, distorted relationships are not, however, the end of the story. God loves us so much that God will not leave us alone in our alienation, separation, and abusive power-over relationships. God continually pursues us to bring about right-relation, to restore us to wholeness and unity with God, with each other, and with the goodness of the world.

To bring about right-relation in the world, God entered into a covenanted relationship with the people of Israel, freeing them from bondage in Egypt. In the Law, God gave the people of Israel a way by which they, and through them all humanity, could be joined anew to God in right-relation. And when the people of Israel strayed from this way of wholeness and restoration, God raised up prophets to remind them that their vocation was to herald and make real God's justice and right-ordered world for all people—to be a light to the nations.

As Christians we believe that God's seeking of right-relation continues beyond God's covenants with the people of Israel, the giving of the Law, and the prophets. We believe that God, in God's love, took a unique and decisive step by choosing to become one of us, by choosing to join us in our pain, suffering, and brokenness. In the incarnation of Jesus, God became one of us so that the walls that divide us and alienate us could forever be torn down. In Jesus, fully human and fully divine, God crossed the boundaries that separate us from God, from other people, and from all creation. God's love in Jesus is all about wholeness, right-relation, and unity—unity with God, unity with each other, unity with creation. Our catechism thus affirms that the mission of the Church (or more appropriately, the *mission of God* in which the Church is privileged to participate) is "to restore all people to unity with God and each other in Christ."[3] God's mission in Jesus is none other than God's action, through the power of the Holy Spirit to effect right-relation in a new creation, to overcome the sinfulness of our disordered and distorted relationships—to make the broken whole.

As the Body of Christ we are called to share in God's action to effect right-relation with God, with other people, and with all creation. Baptism is our commission, co-mission, in God's mission to restore all people to unity with God and each other in Christ. We are called and empowered to be agents of God's restoring love wherever there is brokenness, betrayal and abuse in the world and in the Church, or perhaps especially in the Church. For abuse in the Church seriously undermines our participation in God's mission to restore all people to unity with God and each other in Christ.

This accessible book by my colleague and friend, Robin Hammeal-Urban, is an exercise in effecting wholeness and right-relation. As such it is an invitation to more faithful participation in God's mission of restoration. In it the reader will find helpful and clear actions the church can take to help heal individuals, congregations, and dioceses/judicatories after there has been a betrayal of trust. Robin's clear step-by-step analysis and recommendations, especially with respect to processes of disclosure and truth telling, combined with powerful stories from her own experience as a church official, make this book a highly practical and at the same time readable resource. The appendices containing sample statements and suggested processes for disclosure meetings are helpful for communities and church leaders who might be struggling to discern next steps in the wake of abuse. This book is so much needed in our church and I am delighted that Robin's gifts and experiences are now available to a larger audience.

---

3. Ibid, 855.

I thank God for Robin's collegiality and faithfulness as the Canon for Mission Integrity and Training in the Episcopal Church in Connecticut. For close to fifteen years she has advised and counseled parish lay and ordained leaders, bishops and diocesan committees and councils, in Connecticut and across The Episcopal Church. Her always calm, grounded, and faithful demeanor and wise counsel—especially in times of anxiety and high emotion—have helped countless individuals and communities take the hard steps towards wholeness after betrayal and the reestablishment of trust in the wake of misconduct. Robin's ministry and this book embody and extend God's mission to restore all people to unity with God and each other in Christ.

The Rt. Rev. Ian T. Douglas

INTRODUCTION

magine a church served by a beloved rector. Everyone knows and trusts everyone else. Members describe the congregation as "one big happy family." Last week the rector was involved in a serious car accident. He veered off the road and hit a utility pole on his way home from a restaurant. When police and medics arrived they immediately realized that the rector was intoxicated. The rector is in the hospital recovering from his injuries and will likely be there for another week.

Generally, members are shocked and saddened. They want to know when their rector will return to them and how they can care for him in the meantime. The wardens are not completely surprised. They knew that things weren't going so well. On five previous occasions the wardens were called to come and get the rector from the same restaurant about forty-five minutes out of town; he was too intoxicated to drive. On three of these occasions, he was with a woman from the congregation who was recently widowed. The rector had ministered to her and her husband as he was dying. She is now keeping vigil by the rector's side at the hospital. She intends to care for him in her home upon his discharge from the hospital and indicates, "He practically lives with me."

Since the rector's hospitalization, the wardens, bookkeeper, and church administrator have tried to make sense of the rector's record-keeping. They have discovered that the parish register has not been updated since the bishop's last visitation. When the wardens review a bank statement for the rector's discretionary fund they become concerned, as large amounts of money seem to be flowing through this fund. Their concern has grown as they learn that the bookkeeper has had nothing to do with the discretionary fund, the rector has handled it all, checks have been made out to cash, and the fund has not been audited.

On top of this, a member of the local press called a warden to ask for a comment regarding the rector. During this call the warden learned that the police plan to arrest the rector for driving while intoxicated. The bishop has informed the wardens that when the rector is discharged from the hospital, he will not return to serve in the parish. The rector will need to focus on his well being, attend to criminal proceedings in secular court, and perhaps attend to ecclesiastical disciplinary proceedings.

Members are experiencing a wide range of reactions. Some are angry with the wardens for not having intervened sooner; if they had, the rector could have been spared this recent tragic event. Some are angry with the woman whose husband just died; she should have known that the rector was in a vulnerable state and should not have risked tarnishing his reputation by being seen with him. Some are sad because they believed their church to be perfect—at least one big happy family—and now that image of the church is lost. Some are pooling their funds to pay for the rector's legal expenses, and some are angry with the bishop for taking away their beloved rector and being so "un-pastoral" by not letting the rector return to them in his time of need.

As the week progresses, members are becoming more and more anxious. A number of members are beginning to treat each other harshly. Longtime friends who supported each other through life's challenges cannot support each other now; they find themselves on opposite sides of this situation. Relationships among members are becoming frayed. A few vestry members have resigned because they are so angry with the bishop that they don't want to be part of the church. Interestingly, not many members seem to be angry with the rector—he appears to be the victim in all this. Others are ostracizing the few who are angry with the rector.

This fictitious story may seem extreme, but it is not farfetched. When a congregational leader crosses boundaries, often more than one type of boundary is crossed. Unfortunately, our imaginary rector is in deep trouble—in so many ways. He may be involved in a sexualized relationship with a parishioner. He may have embezzled funds. Moreover, he appears to have a problematic relationship with alcohol and will likely face criminal charges in secular court for driving under the influence. While this story is fictitious, all other scenarios and examples found in these pages are based on real events. Many are amalgams of actual events from congregations across the Church. It is likely that you, the reader, are aware of even more episodes that illustrate the dynamics of misconduct in a congregation.

Almost everyone, whether they attend a church or not, is familiar with instances of misconduct in a church. Consider the following examples: an elected lay leader embezzles church funds to pay for a vacation house and cars for her family; this continues for years before it is detected. A longtime church musician is arrested, convicted, and incarcerated for sexual abuse of children; during his tenure he took youth choirs on international concert tours. A married priest has "an affair"[1] with a recently divorced woman in his congregation; he ministered to her throughout the breakdown of her marriage. A senior warden offers to provide childcare so parents can volunteer at a church function; while trusted with their care, he sexually abuses the children. A respected rector makes romantic overtures to numerous women in his parish and over a dozen of these overtures become fully sexualized relationships while the rector continues to serve the parish. An older priest sexualizes a relationship with a young woman who sought pastoral care and support after the death of her father. A rector uses sexually explicit language during confirmation classes and sexually abuses an adolescent male in the class.

What do all of these examples have in common? A lay or ordained leader has betrayed the trust of a congregation. The leader's persona and position of authority in the church engendered trust, which the leader betrayed by putting his or her own needs before those of the congregation's members. While some congregational misconduct violates secular law, the effects of misconduct can be devastating even if secular law is not violated.

---

1. "Affair" generally connotes a sexualized relationship between two consenting adults. This is not an accurate description of a sexualized relationship between an ordained leader and an individual to whom he or she ministers. The disparity of power between the two individuals diminishes, if not completely negates, the ability of the recipient of ministry to voluntarily consent to a sexualized relationship. For further information and training materials on preventing the exploitation of adults in congregations, see *www.cpg.org/productsservices/ preventingsexualabuse.cfm*.

The fallout from misconduct in a congregation can be devastating to both individual members and the congregation as a community. Restoring trust in oneself, other parishioners, and even God, is difficult work that can be guided, nurtured, and supported by congregational and judicatory leaders. A path toward healing and wholeness for individual members and the congregation is set out in the chapters that follow.

WHY THIS BOOK?

The goal of this book is to offer information and practical step-by-step suggestions to facilitate effective responses to misconduct in congregations. The information and suggestions have been informed, developed, and tested while serving on diocesan staff for the Episcopal Church in Connecticut since 2000. During this time there have been a number of congregations experiencing and struggling with the aftermath of misconduct by ordained and lay leaders. In some congregations the misconduct occurred long before I began to serve on diocesan staff, and yet the effects were still palpable.

My intention is to offer tools that can used by any denomination to build up Christian communities of faith—the Body of Christ. Caring and supporting those who are directly impacted by misconduct—primary victims and those who offend—is important; however, it is equally important to care and support all members of a congregation. It is through this work that members learn to confront their own reactions to misconduct, minister to one another, acknowledge any harm they may have caused others, restore trust with one another, and reconcile relationships with others in the congregation. Doing this work equips members to engage in God's mission of restoration and reconciliation in other settings. This is the work we, as the Church, are called to do. And while it is unclear what our Church will look like in the future, it is clear that healthy Christian communities will continue to be essential in the formation of disciples.

If any of what is within these pages causes distress to anyone who was victimized or impacted by misconduct in a congregation, I apologize for the harm caused by my words and ask your forgiveness. I have sought to treat those who were victimized and those who offend with dignity and respect, while attempting to convey the importance and intricacies of caring for all members of congregations in the wake of misconduct.[2]

LANGUAGE

Throughout this book I use the term *offender* to refer to the person who abused power and violated another, or who is alleged to have violated another. For readability, I did not insert the word "alleged" every time it could be inserted. The offender can be either an ordained or lay leader.

For readability, I use the word *victim* to refer to individuals who were injured, harmed, or wronged by an ordained or lay leader. My use of this word is not meant to imply that any individual is weak, helpless, passive, or powerless. On the contrary, the stories shared in this book are those of victims of misconduct who took action to seek healing for themselves, accountability for the offender, and are survivors of misconduct. The phrase *primary victim(s)* refers to the individual(s) directly impacted/violated by an offender in a congregation, for example, the parishioner with whom the rector engages in a sexualized relationship or the child sexually abused by the choirmaster. Typically, all members of a faith community are impacted by misconduct and are *secondary victims*.

I have intentionally refrained from using of the word "reconciliation" in descriptions of processes to restore trust in congregations. For many primary victims, offenders, and members of congregations, using the word reconciliation in the wake of misconduct triggers incorrect assumptions—that they are being asked to forgive, forget, and become friends again with those who hurt them. While this could be seen as a teachable moment, it is counterproductive to try to teach the theology of reconciliation when people are in the midst of suffering and understandably strong emotional responses. This teaching may be possible when members have moved through much of the healing and restoration process, but can detract from the critical issues that need to be addressed in the immediate wake of misconduct.

---

2. Chapter 11 is devoted to the care and support of primary victims and offenders.

MISCONDUCT BY LAYPERSONS

When I joined the staff of the Episcopal Church in Connecticut, my role was primarily to assist when there were allegations of clergy misconduct. I soon learned that lay leaders also engage in misconduct; in some cases, the impact on the congregation was far greater than if a rector had engaged in the same behavior. Long-serving staff members, or individuals and families who have a lock on parish leadership (often for generations), can amass more power and trust within the parish system than a rector. Betrayal of trust by a lay leader can be devastating to a congregation.

Examples and responses to lay misconduct are provided. Almost all processes described in this book, even if they only refer to clergy misconduct, can be modified to respond to lay misconduct. While the disciplinary canons of the Episcopal Church do not apply to lay misconduct, within the confines of diocesan canons a disciplinary process for lay misconduct can be created. The ecclesiastical authority for such a process is typically the rector.

DISCIPLINARY CANONS IN THE EPISCOPAL CHURCH

As of the writing of this book, the disciplinary process for clergy in the Episcopal Church is set out in Title IV of the Canons. These canons were significantly changed at General Convention in 2009 and modified in 2012. The significant changes, which went into effect as of July 1, 2011, shifted the disciplinary process from one of retributive justice (based on military law) to a process based on restorative justice, more closely aligned with our call as Christians. It is likely that these canons will be revised at subsequent General Conventions as our experiences with disciplinary proceedings become more informed over time.

This book is not a guide to the canonical disciplinary processes and should not be relied on as such.[3] Rather, it is a guide to working with congregations to restore trust in the wake of misconduct. References to canons are included in boxes within the text where

---

3. For training materials on the disciplinary processes and proceedings set out in Title IV, consult the website for the Episcopal Church in Connecticut at *www.episcopalct.org*.

canons directly address this work. The content of this book, which focuses on human reactions and dynamics in congregations, will remain valid and relevant even if the canons undergo another significant revision.[4]

OTHER DENOMINATIONS

Although written with a focus on the Episcopal Church, this book addresses congregational dynamics and the work to restore trust among those impacted by misconduct. These human dynamics are universal regardless of a congregation's denomination. The processes set out can be translated for use by judicatory and/or congregational leaders in other denominations. Some processes may need to be modified to reflect differences in polity.

For those unfamiliar with the structure and roles in Episcopal congregations, a brief description of some of the key terminology used throughout this book follows. A congregation in the Episcopal Church is referred to as a *parish, congregation,* or *mission.* Parishes within a proscribed geographic area are connected to each other to form a *diocese.* Ordained and lay leaders in each diocese elect a *bishop*—the judicatory leader. The bishop is charged with the care of clergy and congregations, and has specific responsibility and authority within the canonical disciplinary process.

Parish leadership generally consists of a *rector*, an ordained leader called to serve a congregation. This is a tenured position.[5] The *wardens* are lay leaders, elected by members to serve the congregation. There are two wardens who are among the officers of the parish. In the absence of ordained leadership, the responsibility of running the day-to-day life of the parish is the wardens'. A *vestry* is a group of lay leaders elected by members of the parish to lead the parish with the ordained leader. Among other things, a vestry has responsibility for budgeting and overseeing the funds of the church.

---

4. At the time of this writing, there is no indication that the disciplinary canons will undergo a significant revision.

5. Some churches have an *interim rector, vicar,* or *priest-in-charge* instead of a rector. These are ordained leadership roles that do not have tenure.

The *chancellor* is the bishop's attorney. One of the chancellor's roles is to counsel the bishop and seek to protect the legal interests of the judicatory. A *parish attorney* is an attorney, who may or may not be a member of the parish, who counsels parish leaders and seeks to protect the legal interests of the parish. The chancellor and parish attorney are two separate roles; they cannot be served by the same person.

BLESSINGS AND CALL

As Christians we are called to share the love of Christ and work to reconcile the brokenness of this world. Brokenness exists, on many levels, in the wake of misconduct. The work of accompanying and shepherding congregations through processes to restore trust is hard work; it takes stamina, faith, perseverance, and emotional and spiritual health.

This work is best approached as a form of art, rather than a formulaic process. It reflects a kind of dance between following the steps of appropriately tailored processes and making room for the power and grace of the Holy Spirit, through whom the real work of restoration and transformation is possible. The blessing of accompanying and shepherding congregations in the wake of misconduct is a privilege. It is an honor, and humbling, to be present in the midst of pain and brokenness, and to witness holy moments of transformation. I pray that all who engage in this work will recognize the blessings in the midst of the challenges.

Robin Hammeal-Urban
Lent 2015
East Hampton, Connecticut

1

A Betrayal of Trust

MISCONDUCT

God is at work in the world. The work of the Church is to join in God's mission to reconcile the brokenness of this world to God's ever-present love. Much of this work and witness of Christ's love is carried out by members of congregations. Regardless of variations in polity among denominations, the hearts, voices, hands, and feet of Christ are those of the members of congregations who witness the love and transformative power of our Lord and Savior, Jesus Christ.

To witness and be the presence of Christ on earth, members of congregations need to *know*, in their core being, the love and transformative power of Christ. To *know* this transformative love can be unsettling. It can challenge the rational, logical precepts and values of our dominant culture. It can turn one's plans upside down. It can shake the foundations of people's lives.

When congregations are trustworthy communities of faith, they can invite members to truly know the transformative power of Christ; hardness of heart and closed-minded thinking can be gently softened and pried open by trust. In healthy, vital congregations, members trust one another; they share their whole being, including their brokenness, with God and each other. Churches should be safe places for members to be wholly honest with one another, revealing who one really is in a world where that is rarely safe to do. Trust is essential for spiritual growth.

Members trust their leaders to act in the best interests of the congregation regardless of whether the leader was elected, called, or placed in a leadership position by a judicatory leader. It is this trust that creates an opportunity for members to be vulnerable when seeking a closer relationship with God. Often this trust runs deep.

At its core, congregational misconduct is a betrayal of trust by a leader who puts his or her needs before those of the people to whom he or she ministers.[1] In essence, the leader abuses the power bestowed by virtue of holding a position of leadership in a church. The opportunity to commit congregational misconduct arises from this trust. The trusted leader can be an ordained or a lay minister.

THE CHARACTERISTICS OF BETRAYAL

Many of us have experienced betrayal in our lives; a friend violates a confidence, a family member hides an addiction by creating stories to "cover up" the addictive behavior, a business partner or employee embezzles funds, a spouse engages in an affair. Betrayal occurs when a person we trust acts in ways that are not compatible with the person we believe him or her to be. The depth of betrayal depends on the level of intimacy and trust in the relationship. Betrayal is not new. People have been betraying one another for thousands of years. All people are fallible. All of us have the potential to betray those who trust us.

The pain from being wronged by a friend or a loved one is far greater and more complicated than the pain that flows from being wronged by a stranger. The Bible is full of examples of betrayal in both the Old and New Testaments. Consider the angst and pain expressed in Psalm 55:

It is not enemies who taunt me—
    I could bear that;
it is not adversaries who deal
        insolently with me—
    I could hide from them.

---

1. See the disciplinary canons, Title IV.3 and IV.4, regarding accountability and standards of conduct for ordained leaders in the Episcopal Church.

But it is you, my equal,
>   my companion, my familiar
>   friend,
>   with whom I kept pleasant
>   company;
>   we walked in the house of God
>   with the throng. . . .
> My companion laid hands on a
>   friend
> and violated a covenant
>   with me
> with speech smoother than
>   butter,
>   but with a heart set on war;
> with words that were softer
>   than oil,
>   but in fact were drawn swords.[2]

For the psalmist, the pain would be bearable if the wrongdoer were an "enemy." However, the wrongdoer was not an enemy, but a trusted companion.

SECRETIVE NATURE OF BETRAYAL

Betrayal typically involves secrecy; things are made to look one way when in reality, something quite different is going on. A person betraying another may go to great lengths to "cover up" his or her actions or intentions. The psalmist's friend spoke "as smooth as butter" and used words that were "softer than oil," while concealing a "heart set on war."

The pain of betrayal is exacerbated by the secretive nature of betrayal. Secrecy and cover-up makes it hard to know where the truth lies. Secrecy makes reality hard to perceive. The difficulty in perceiving reality is twofold: first, the cover-up and secrecy make

---

2. Psalm 55:12–14; 20–21.

it hard to know where reality begins and ends, and second, no one wants to experience the pain that comes with discovering that they have been betrayed. In essence, the effort to avoid the pain of realizing that one has been betrayed combines with the struggle to find reality in the midst of the lies, misinformation, incomplete truths, and cover-ups.

IMPERCEPTIBILITY OF BETRAYAL

Few of us want to "see" or acknowledge that we have been betrayed. This "not wanting to see" is the same dynamic that causes parishioners not to report warning signs when a church school teacher is sexually abusing a child. This phenomenon has been summed up as, "if it's inconceivable, it's unperceivable." This means that "[w]hen an event is inconceivable it's also unperceivable. . . . Because it's inconceivable to all of us that someone we know, maybe even like or admire or respect or trust, could actually sexually abuse a child. And because we can't conceive it, our minds won't allow us to perceive it, even in the face of compelling evidence!"[3]

Thus, for some members of congregations it is inconceivable that a trusted leader could commit misconduct; they cannot perceive the wrongful acts even when confronted with evidence. For them, like the psalmist, the pain of betrayal is unbearable. It is too painful to face. These members may continue to believe that their trust was, and is, well placed in the offender. Other members will believe that the misconduct occurred, feel the pain of betrayal, and question their ability to assess who is trustworthy.

There will be members who vacillate between entertaining the possibility that misconduct occurred and believing that the trusted leader would never engage in such behavior. It is essential that congregations find ways to embrace all members regardless of differences in their experiences of misconduct. To help a faith community come to terms with congregational misconduct, members need accurate, timely information about the transgression(s) and opportunities to process that information as a community.

---

3. Praesidium Safety Bulletin, *www.praesidiuminc.com/bulletin/bulletin_vol_16.php#PraesidiumProductSpotlight*, November 2009.

THE PREVALENCE OF CONGREGATIONAL MISCONDUCT

Unfortunately, congregational misconduct is not a rare occurrence. The frequency of misconduct is astounding; the cases most widely reported by the press involve the sexual abuse of children by trusted ordained and lay leaders. Most people can name a church or ordained leader they knew who was implicated, in some way, of this horrific crime.

While clergy sexual misconduct (CSM) with adults does not receive the same attention in the media, it is widespread. A 2009 study of the prevalence of CSM "refute[s] the commonly held belief that it is a case of a few charismatic and powerful leaders preying on vulnerable followers."[4] This Baylor University study found that "more than 3% of women who had attended a congregation in the past month reported that they had been the object of CSM at some time in their adult lives; 92% of these sexual advances had been made in secret, not in open dating relationships; and 67% of the offenders were married to someone else at the time of the advance."[5] Notably, these numbers reflect the rate of CSM experienced by women who continue to participate in congregational life. Many women who experience CSM are unable to bring themselves to attend worship in any church.

Examining these statistics reveals that "[i]n the average American congregation of 400 persons . . . there are on average 7 women who have experienced CSM [as primary victims and]. . . . there are, on average, 32 persons who have experienced CSM in their community of faith [as secondary victims or bystanders.]"[6] When one considers the personal connections of each of these people—connections with family, friends, and colleagues—the effects of misconduct expand exponentially to include other individuals and their communities of faith.

No denomination or faith is immune to CSM. In the Baylor University study, the "survivors [of CSM] hailed from 17 different Christian and Jewish affiliations: Catholic, Baptist, Methodist, Lutheran,

---

4. The Prevalence of Clergy Sexual Misconduct with Adults: A Research Study Executive Summary, *www.baylor.edu/clergysexualmisconduct/index.php?id=67406*, 2009.

5. *Ibid.*

6. *Ibid.*

Seventh Day Adventist, Disciples of Christ, Latter Day Saints, Apostolic, Calvary Chapel, Christian Science, Church of Christ, Episcopal, Friends (Quaker), Mennonite, Evangelical, Nondenominational (Christian), and Reform Judaism."[7]

Financial misconduct in congregations is also a relatively common occurrence. In 2006, the Center for the Study of Church Management at Villanova University conducted a study of the 174 Catholic dioceses in the United States. The chief financial officers of seventy-eight dioceses responded to the research inquiry, and "85% of the respondents acknowledged serious problems [in their parishes] in the five previous years. While 27% of respondents reported less than $50,000 in embezzlements, 11% claimed embezzlements totaling more than $500,000 and the rest were somewhere in between."[8] When asked why embezzlement occurs in churches, Chuck Zech, director of the Center for the Study of Church Management, replied: "Churches are too busy trusting. . . . They're more like families. People can't imagine their fellow parishioner would be stealing."[9] Embezzlement readily reveals the monetary costs of congregational misconduct. However, there are other "costs" which often exceed the monetary costs.

THE FAR-REACHING EFFECTS
OF CONGREGATIONAL MISCONDUCT

Betrayal can occur in any human relationship. When it occurs in a church, its effects are widespread. By its very nature, misconduct in a community of faith is not a private matter between those directly impacted—the offender and primary victim(s).

The following is a list of individuals and groups most often affected by congregational misconduct. Of course, such a list is not exhaustive.

- The offender
- The offender's partner/spouse, children, and extended family

---

7. *Ibid.*
8. *www.uscatholic.org/church/2009/04/collection-racket?page=0%262*
9. *Ibid.*

- Primary victim(s)
- Primary victim's partner/spouse, children, and extended family
- Friends of both the offender and primary victim(s)
- Staff of the congregation
- Lay leaders
- Adult members
- Youth members
- Children of the congregation
- Judicatory leaders: bishop and others responsible for responding to misconduct
- Other churches within the community
- Other clergy within the same denomination (if the offender is ordained)
- Clergy in other denominations
- Members of other churches within the same denomination
- Members of churches in other denominations
- People who are not members of any community of faith
- Future ordained and lay leaders of the church

In addition, the reputation of the church where the misconduct occurred, and indeed the reputation of all churches, can be affected.

The Impact on Members and the Faith Community

Reactions to congregational misconduct occur on two levels, individually for each member and corporately as a community. How individual members react can vary greatly and is often affected by each member's life experiences. These reactions include:

- **Anger** at the bishop or the authority imposing discipline on the offender, at the primary victim(s), at other members for allowing this to happen, at oneself for not seeing the warning signs, and at the offender. Notably, anger at the offender who was, or is, a trusted leader can be a delayed reaction due to the complexity of betrayal.

- **Blaming the victim** for the misconduct or for revealing it.

- **Blaming one's self** for having a role in placing the offender in a position of leadership which provided opportunity to engage in misconduct, *e.g.*, serving on the search/calling committee, or having actively sought to have the person elected or selected.

- **Shame** for being affiliated with a church where misconduct occurred.

- **Disbelief** that a trusted leader could do something harmful, or that this is happening in their own church.

- **Loss and grief,** on many levels. Loss for the way things were before the misconduct; loss of the image of the church as perfect, or from disappointment in how the church responded to misconduct. In addition, trusting relationships among members may be broken, resulting in additional loss.

- **Opening old wounds** from prior experiences of betrayal, loss, victimization, or other trauma. Such prior experiences may have occurred in a church setting or elsewhere. As one church member described it, the grief and loss in the wake of misconduct felt like the grief of losing her husband seven years earlier.

- **Internal conflict** in knowing that the offender engaged in good ministry and also committed misconduct. It is often difficult for members to hold both realities at once—that the leader engaged in extraordinary ministry while also engaging in misconduct. Facing the reality that all of us have the capacity to do both good and evil can be difficult.

- **Erosion of trust** in other relationships is common; members' ability and willingness to trust others erodes. This can affect relationships in and beyond the congregation, and one's relationship with God. The resulting anguish can be deep.

- **Lack of trust in one's self** can flow from having been betrayed by someone deeply trusted. If a member's intuition or "gut feeling" indicated that a leader was trustworthy, the revelation that he or she was not can raise doubts about one's ability to assess trustworthiness. The ability to trust one's own intuition may be diminished.

- **Lack of trust in other members** who encouraged trust in the offender or also trusted the offender.
- **Lack of trust of clergy,** even those who have never committed any type of misconduct.
- **Lack of trust in God** or one's understanding and perception of God.

An individual member may find himself or herself reacting differently at different times. Efforts to care for congregations in the wake of misconduct need to take into account all of these varied reactions. Such efforts must seek to ensure that all members are treated with dignity and respect, regardless of each member's reaction to the misconduct.

Just as individual members react to misconduct, so too congregations as communities react. The consequences of misconduct in a congregation can be profound and continue for generations. The erosion of trust, like ripples from a stone thrown into a still pond, can extend to all members of the congregation and beyond.

Often there is division within the congregation between members who support the offender and those who support the primary victim(s). This division can be deep. (It can mirror the internal conflict of individual members who struggle with knowing and accepting that the offender did wonderful ministry and, yet, committed misconduct.) Members who have been friends for years may suddenly find themselves on different sides of this painful issue; those who supported one another during difficult times may suddenly seem like strangers. The faith community that once felt familiar and safe now feels foreign. Relationships among members are strained; some are broken.

In an effort to support the offender, members may withhold their financial support from the church. Sometimes members divert their funds to assist the offender with living expenses or legal fees. Congregational membership may decline.

There can be an unhealthy disparity of power among members. Information and knowledge is power. Members who have information about the misconduct will have more power in the congregation than those who do not. Those who gain power by having this information may seek to control the flow of information in an effort to protect others or in an attempt to secure power for themselves. The members with information may not be elected leaders or those who legitimately hold authority in the congregation. Those who do not have complete and accurate information about misconduct may fill in the gaps by speculating as to what happened. Members may share such speculation with each other. Speculation may be repeated as rumor and understood as fact.

Even if some members do not know what happened, those members (and even newcomers) will know that *something* has happened. If the misconduct is not addressed openly and honestly in a timely manner, it sends the message that there are certain things not to be spoken of within the congregation. Members may become careful about what information they share; they begin to self-censor. From a theological viewpoint, this may be one of the most devastating effects of congregational misconduct—members no longer bring their own brokenness to God through their faith community because painful topics are not addressed within the community. Direct communication decreases and triangulation increases.

The feelings experienced by individual members (as discussed above) will be present in the life of the congregation. These feelings may be displaced and misdirected at other members and leaders during fellowship events, committee meetings, or even worship. Inappropriate displays of anger are not uncommon following misconduct. When leaders or members of a congregation engage in yelling, name calling, fist pounding, and storming out of meetings, the reason for these behaviors is often something other than the topic under discussion. Typically, a look back at the congregation's history will reveal a critical betrayal of trust.

Often, ordained leaders serving in congregations immediately after misconduct are not trusted or accepted by the members. These clergy, referred to as *afterpastors*, face serious challenges. Even when a skilled afterpastor serves a congregation, the lack of trust and acceptance can result in high turnover and upheaval in ordained leadership. These transitions can be traumatic for a congregation. This is especially true if the leave taking of the afterpastor is not done well. "Leaving well" requires both the ordained leader and the congregation to be able to recognize the gifts and challenges of their ministry together, and to bring closure to their relationship in a healthy manner.

In the wake of misconduct, there is often a sense of separateness, broken relationships among members, unhealthy power differentials, secret keeping, and displaced anger. When not properly addressed, these dynamics can be handed down from one generation to the next. Without a timely and appropriate response to the misconduct, these unhealthy dynamics can become the way a congregation operates for decades.

A Case Study

The following case study illustrates the complexity and diversity of issues that arise from misconduct and the challenges to restoring right relationship among members.

> Imagine a parish served by a priest who is deeply loved by the congregation. He provides wonderful pastoral care and inspired preaching. He has a cheery disposition. (The former priest did not.) He openly admits that he doesn't understand much about finances and leaves that for lay leaders to manage. During much of his tenure, the same three people serve as wardens and treasurer; all three are members of families who have been pillars in the congregation for generations. Brief financial reports are provided to the vestry on an irregular basis.
>
> After twenty years of caring for the congregation, the priest retires. The wardens collect a large cash purse for the retiring rector, and his farewell celebration is glorious. Within a few months, a new priest arrives. Coincidentally, all three of the key lay leaders leave the congregation or die within a few months of the new priest's arrival. There aren't other lay leaders ready to step into their shoes.
>
> As the new priest starts to settle in, she begins to review minutes from vestry meetings and the brief financial reports. She finds that standard money counting practices, internal controls, and auditing procedures were not followed. Almost all of the church's financial transactions were done on a cash basis. There are few records of expenditures other than checks made out to "Cash." The financial

reports that were provided to the vestry and congregation do not seem to correlate with any of the supporting financial documents.

A forensic audit reveals that over $230,000 cannot be accounted for. This money may well have been spent on appropriate church expenses, but this can't be documented. Members start to speculate that perhaps the three lay leaders used the money to buy the new cars that each of them acquired within the last few years. Only some members know about the forensic audit. The new priest thinks it would be best if the entire parish did *not* know because she wants to move forward on a strategic plan.

Imagine how it would feel to be a member of this congregation. There is a swirl of reactions, emotions and thoughts; some members have accurate information about the finances, others do not. The feelings and reactions of members may include some of the following:

- Bewilderment
- Anger at the former priest for letting them so deeply trust the three lay leaders
- Anger at the three lay leaders
- Anger at other members for expressing negative thoughts about the three lay leaders as those leaders did so much good for the church, and/or because they are related to them by blood or marriage
- Anger at people who served on the vestry for not having kept a closer eye on the money
- Anger at the new priest for raising the issue: "Everything was just fine before *she* arrived."
- Anger because other people are angry
- Self-blame for not asking more questions sooner
- Impatience (These are members who just want to "move forward.")
- Loss of image of their church as being perfect
- Sadness
- Division

This is a complicated situation. Instances of congregational misconduct typically are. There may be more than one wrongdoer. There may be shared culpability. Members may start to point fingers at one another. At this stage, not all of the facts are known. It may be impossible to ever fully account for the entire $230,000. What we do know is that currently, it is very unlikely that this community of faith can nurture spiritual growth among its members and bring the Good News of Christ to the world.

Trust must be reestablished among the members for this community to grow into a healthy vital congregation. Members need to move toward reconciliation with one another. For this to occur, all members need accurate, timely information about the possible misconduct. In addition, they need to find ways to hold each other in Christian community even while experiencing different and perhaps opposing feelings and reactions to the possible misconduct.

The focus of caring for congregations in the wake of misconduct is not to seek reconciliation with the offender, but rather to rebuild the faith community so that it and its members can witness Christ's transformative love and power in the world. Reconciliation with the offender may be an additional blessing or outcome of this work, but it is not the focus.

Speaking the Truth

DISCLOSURE

We are called to speak the truth about misconduct in our congregations. God created us, loves us, and cares for us. God created us to be in right relationship with God and each other. We experience this, in part, through Christian fellowship. Early Christians "devoted themselves to the apostles' teaching and fellowship, to the breaking of bread and the prayers."[1] Christian fellowship is not merely companionship; it is a deeper level of connectedness. God is at the center of this fellowship. Each individual is connected to God, through Christ, and is thereby connected with all believers. Healthy faith communities nurture discipleship by providing members with an incarnate experience of Christian fellowship—the experience of being in right relationship with others. This requires us to be authentic and speak truthfully to one another.

Numerous passages in both the Old and New Testaments urge us to be truthful.

One of the most familiar admonitions regarding truthfulness in the Old Testament is the eighth commandment: "You shall not bear false witness against your neighbor."[2] We learn from Proverbs that, "Truthful lips endure forever, but a lying tongue lasts only a moment."[3] Psalm 120 proclaims:

---

1. Acts 2:42.
2. Exodus 20:16.
3. Proverbs 12:19.

Deliver me, O Lord,
> from lying lips,
> from a deceitful tongue.

What shall be given to you?
> And what more shall be done
> > to you,
> you deceitful tongue?

A warrior's sharp arrows,
> with glowing coals of the
> > broom tree![4]

In the New Testament we learn that being truthful requires more than simply not lying—it requires us to refrain from hiding; it requires us to disclose the truth. By failing to disclose truths, we are in essence lying by omission. According to Mark, Jesus said, "Is a lamp brought in to be put under the bushel basket, or under the bed, and not on the lampstand? For there is nothing hidden, except to be disclosed; nor is anything secret, except to come to light."[5] Similarly, according to Luke, Jesus told his disciples, "Beware of the yeast of the Pharisees, that is, their hypocrisy. Nothing is covered up that will not be uncovered, and nothing secret that will not become known. Therefore whatever you have said in the dark will be heard in the light, and what you have whispered behind closed doors will be proclaimed from the housetops."[6]

Hypocrisy and secrets are to be brought into the light. Perhaps this is what propels victims of misconduct to tell church authorities about abuse even decades after the abuse has ended—they need to bring the secret to light in order to heal and restore right relationships with others and God.

For our relationships to be authentic and trustworthy, we need to know the truth about ourselves and others. This is particularly true for all members of congregations who have been betrayed by a trusted leader, lay or ordained. Misconduct erodes trust, not

---

4. Psalm 120:2–4.

5. Mark 4:21–22.

6. Luke 12:1–3.

only between the offender and primary victim, but also among other members of a congregation. To begin to rebuild or establish trust, it is essential that misconduct, which typically involves secrets and secretive behavior, be disclosed and brought to light. To create right relationships among ourselves and with God, we need to know our brokenness and injurious actions. All people and situations can be redeemed in Christ. This redemption is not possible when there are secrets or lack of awareness of wrongdoing by oneself and others.

FOUR LEVELS OF DISCLOSURE

As Christians, we are called to tell about misconduct in our congregations on the *intrapersonal*, *interpersonal*, *institutional*, and *cultural* levels.[7] Communicating accurate information, or telling the truth about what has been secret, can be transformative and healing to many when all four of these levels are addressed.

To illustrate the four levels and how they interact, consider the example of addiction to alcohol or other drugs. When the brokenness of addiction is addressed on all four levels—intrapersonal, interpersonal, institutional, and cultural—healing and restoration to wholeness is possible for those directly impacted and beyond.

Bringing the secret of addiction to light requires recognition that there is a secret or something hidden on an *intra*personal level. Many struggle to see and recognize their own brokenness within, which underlies their addiction. On an *inter*personal level, friends and family members may not want to see this brokenness even if the person struggling with addiction sees and speaks of it. These friends and relatives may resist the truth and continue to live with the truth hidden—in the dark. *Institutions* such as schools, workplaces, political structures, and even churches may have practices that encourage the consumption of alcohol or other drugs to enhance productivity, solidify relationships (for example the martini lunch

---

7. These four levels are part of the multicultural process of change as articulated by Dr. Valerie Batts, co-founder and executive director of Visions, Inc., *www.visions-inc.org*. These levels are more fully described in *God's Tapestry: Understanding and Celebrating Differences* by William M. Kondrath (Herndon, VA: Alban Institute, 2008).

or certain networking opportunities), or discourage recognition of addiction when an individual is an asset to the institution. Institutions may engage in these practices even when there are policies stating otherwise.

On the *cultural* level, there are competing messages and values regarding the abuse of alcohol or other drugs. While the messages of "don't drink and drive" and the proliferation of 12-step recovery groups promote responsible consumption of alcohol and recovery, there are competing messages and values in society. Excessive alcohol or drug consumption is portrayed as acceptable or even desirable in situation comedies, movies, and by some celebrities.

Speaking the truth on any of the four levels can encourage recognition of the truth on other levels. Revealing the truth can begin on any level and is an essential step toward wholeness.

Intrapersonal Disclosure

As with addiction, victims of misconduct may struggle on an *intrapersonal* level to recognize that they have in fact been harmed. Denial serves to protect all of us from seeing deep brokenness, until we are able and ready to see it. Victims see and recognize how they have been harmed and the resulting brokenness when they are ready to see it.

As one woman reported, "At first it was a comfort to have the companionship and attention of the priest who had been with me and my husband during my husband's battle with cancer and death. It felt strange when we became lovers, but I was in a daze. It wasn't until months into our relationship that I woke up one day and said to myself, 'Wait, this isn't right.' I was overwhelmed with anger at the priest and fear of what others would think."

In some cases, years can pass before a person can see that a trusted church leader victimized him or her. This "seeing" on an intrapersonal level is most often the first step toward healing from the brokenness and shame of victimization. Those who witness or are bystanders to misconduct may experience a similar process. Often these individuals don't immediately recognize the misconduct. Their awareness may start as an uneasy feeling. Over time, often by gaining additional information, bystanders begin to acknowledge to themselves that their trust has been betrayed.

INTERPERSONAL DISCLOSURE

On an *interpersonal* level, we are led and called to tell other people about our victimization. While some victims achieve a certain level of healing through individual prayer and their personal relationship with God, many do not. In part, this may be because misconduct in a congregation can undermine trust in God. In part, it may be that the Holy Spirit is at work and moves us to share our burdens with others.

Disclosing to another person that we were harmed, and being heard and supported by another, is a significant step toward healing and wholeness. For some, a necessary step for healing is to tell church officials about the misconduct. In essence, they need to tell and confront the institution in which the misconduct occurred.

INSTITUTIONAL DISCLOSURE

The church, as an institution, needs to define, name, respond, and disclose misconduct in congregations and beyond. Many denominations have processes that define misconduct by an ordained leader. In addition to defining, naming, and responding to misconduct, the church is called to tell about misconduct. The church is the community of the New Covenant of which all baptized persons are members; it is one Body of which Jesus Christ is the Head. This community, the Church, cannot be true and authentic if it fails to speak openly and disclose misconduct. Congregational misconduct reflects the human shortcomings of its members—in theological terms, sin.

The Episcopal Church's disciplinary canons define, name, and set out a response to allegations of clergy misconduct. The response to misconduct by lay leaders is not proscribed by canon and this response varies greatly. Yet the harm from misconduct by a trusted lay leader can be as great as that from an ordained leader.

The Episcopal Church's canons grant bishops authority to disclose information concerning an offense or alleged offense as the bishop deems pastorally appropriate. In such disclosures, bishops are to consider the "respective privacy interests and pastoral needs of all affected persons."[8]

CULTURAL DISCLOSURE

On a *cultural* level the Church is called to proclaim and reflect gospel values that may differ from the values of our dominant culture. The Church needs to name the brokenness from abuse and betrayal in relationships, within its walls and beyond. This naming and disclosing is essential if the Church is to teach another way of being, and offer salvation and redemption through Christ.

Consider a congregation where a married rector was having a sexualized relationship with a female parishioner to whom he provided pastoral care during her recent divorce proceedings. During the bishop's initial meeting with the wardens and some vestry members, it was revealed that each lay leader present had engaged in at least one extramarital affair. The disciplinary action that focused on the rector's behavior became an opportunity for the congregation to explore Christian marriage, create opportunities for people to amend their lives, and offer forgiveness for burdens that some had carried for years. The cultural message, that it was the norm to engage in extramarital relationships, was challenged.

RESISTANCE TO DISCLOSURE

There are many impediments and sources of resistance to disclosing misconduct. To overcome this resistance, the impediments need to be recognized, named, explored, and mitigated. This allows leaders to make informed decisions about how best to move forward. Without naming and exploring sources of resistance, a congregation can

---

8. Title IV.6.10; 7.9; 8.3; 8.4; and 14.13.

become stuck and remain fearful of speaking the truth. Some of the more common sources of resistance include:

- **Denial.** For reasons already discussed, it is very difficult and painful to see that a trusted leader has betrayed a congregation. Even when presented with evidence, there will be some members who are unable to accept that they have been betrayed.

- **Fear.** On both an individual and a corporate level, fear can prevent members from recognizing opportunities for new life in the midst of misconduct. This fear may be expressed as concerns that speaking of misconduct will hurt the church, people will leave, pledges will decrease, and people will be hurt. If not addressed, fear can result in keeping secrets about misconduct.

- **Rationalization.** We all know of institutions that close down communication when things go wrong. Consider the college professor who suddenly goes on a terminal sabbatical and is thanked for his or her service and contribution to the college, or the accountant who is immediately escorted out of the office upon sudden termination of employment. Other employees learn by email notification that the accountant's employment has ended and are urged not to discuss the matter. It is essential to remember that unlike the Church, no other organization, whether for profit or nonprofit, charitable, civic, or community based, is called to live out the Gospel as Christ's presence in the world. This requires us to create and nurture communities of Christian fellowship; this calls for a different response.

- **Shame and guilt.** Members may be concerned that they will feel shame if others outside the congregation find out about the misconduct. Others may experience guilt for not having seen or responded to warning signs, or for their role or complicity in the misconduct.

- **Ignoring the true cause.** More often than not, concerns about disclosing misconduct will be expressed as fear and anger toward the person or institution advocating for disclosure. This might sound like, "If you tell the congregation, you will start a firestorm" or "If you tell the congregation, people will leave and we'll lose pledge income." These statements ignore the reality that the makings of the "firestorm" already exist; they were created by the leader's misconduct. Blaming the person or authority promoting disclosure is hiding from reality. Moreover, hoping that the truth stays hidden underestimates a congregation's ability to respond to challenges with appropriate education and support.

THE CONSEQUENCES OF FAILING TO DISCLOSE

The consequences of failing to disclose misconduct to members of a congregation are far reaching and long lasting. Some congregations struggle with the aftermath of hidden misconduct for decades.

ONE CONGREGATION'S STORY

At a monthly vestry meeting, members engaged in a loud emotional conversation. Members were dismissive to and belittling of each other. References were made to prior actions and decisions of members that had not produced the expected results as justification for not listening to that member now. And what was the urgent issue? They were deciding what color to paint the interior of the parish hall!

Upon further examination over a period of weeks, it was discovered that more than twenty-three years ago a rector had sexualized relationships with a number of women in the parish. At that time, a few of the women had shared their stories with selective members of congregation. Each woman who shared her story with other members heard that she was at fault for the sexualized relationship with the rector, that it was the woman's responsibility to stop the relationship and establish appropriate boundaries, or that it was good the rector had someone to lean on since his wife was often unavailable due to her professional demands. None of these women knew there were other women in the congregation who had fallen prey to the rector's misconduct.

While no one spoke openly of the sexualized relationships, there were members who saw things they did not approve of, others who knew instinctively that something wasn't right, and others who whispered about what was going on and feared the fallout if anyone found out—in essence, many members knew something was going on and had different degrees of accurate information. Since this rector's retirement, no priest has served the parish for longer than four years; each tenure was conflicted. No priest was trusted. Members who have joined the congregation in the last twenty years have learned the cultural norms of the congregation and have perpetuated the reactive behaviors.

ANOTHER CONGREGATION'S STORY

A newly ordained assistant rector failed to fulfill the professional responsibilities set out in the job description. There was no Lenten program, no offerings for adult formation, and perhaps most distressing, hospital visits to church members were not made. The assistant spent time befriending wealthy parishioners, overstepping boundaries with female parishioners facing life crises, and intruding into personal lives of members by giving advice (in person and from the pulpit), even when parishioners specifically asked the assistant to have no further involvement in their lives. The assistant received valuable gifts of cash and items from some parishioners. The assistant was seen with different women from the church in settings that created the appearance they were a couple. Many members knew something wasn't right. They began to express concerns to the rector and vestry members.

The rector and vestry decided to terminate the assistant's employment. The assistant hired an attorney and threatened to sue the church for wrongful termination of employment, defamation, libel, and slander.[9] The vestry was afraid of legal action. They agreed to pay a severance package, not disclose the real reasons for the termination, and to issue a statement that read, "Our assistant rector feels called to serve God in a new setting. It is with reluctance and gratitude that your rector and vestry accept this resignation."

---

9. In general terms, defamation is sharing anything that is harmful to the reputation of another. If the information is true, its truthfulness can be raised as a defense to any claim based on defamation. Libel is when such information is shared by publication—in writing. This includes any pictures, images, or text. Slander is when such information is shared orally, through spoken communication.

In exchange, the assistant signed an agreement waiving all rights to sue the church regarding any aspect of employment.

Members of the congregation had questions that remained unanswered: "Why was a severance package paid when the assistant resigned?" "I heard that the assistant was out to dinner at the new fancy French restaurant with Mary (a member). Is that true? Isn't that kind of weird?" "I gave our assistant a handsome cash gift to ensure a smooth transition into our church. Why didn't you tell me that he was resigning? When did you first know? You must have known for a while. It would have been nice if you told me so I could have saved that money and spent it in other ways to support our church."

Six months later the rector, wardens, and vestry asked to meet with the bishop. They were tired and discouraged. They could not get any traction in new initiatives or goals they tried to set for the parish. On the whole, the parish was still focused on unresolved issues regarding the former assistant and seemed to lack trust in the leadership—who couldn't speak about the circumstance surrounding the assistant's departure due to the legally binding confidentiality agreement. They were stuck.

As these examples illustrate, some of the consequences of failing to disclose misconduct are wide ranging and long lasting. Unacceptable behavior continues and is concealed or condoned by silence; trust is not restored and continues to erode; energy is spent ignoring and hiding the truth rather than engaging in mission and ministry; formation of disciples is curtailed as members become reluctant to speak of their individual brokenness because the community does not have the capacity to speak of the brokenness within itself; and primary victims are blamed due to a lack of understanding of the power dynamics in ministerial relationships—they feel unheard.

Moreover, failing to disclose misconduct in a congregation denies others an opportunity to recognize their victimization (in the church or in other settings) and heal from such victimization. It denies the congregation an opportunity to be educated and establish healthy boundaries and systems of checks and accountability. It also creates a power differential between those with knowledge and those without: some members know what is going on; others know something is going on, but do not have accurate information.

Displaced residual anger, sadness, and distrust are common long-term effects of failing to disclose misconduct. This happens when there is no opportunity for members to process their varied experiences and reactions; unspoken and unresolved feelings impact members' behavior. These effects can continue long after the offender has left the congregation. This can be prevented (or minimized) by disclosing information about the misconduct; by educating on power, boundaries, and accountability in ministerial relationships and providing opportunities for members to share how they were impacted. This sharing among members allows them to understand, support, and minister to each other, as well as begin to establish trust among each other.

IT IS NEVER TOO LATE FOR DISCLOSURE

It is never too late to speak the truth about misconduct. The purpose of disclosing misconduct in congregations is to provide opportunity for the restoration of right relationship among members—not to keep the focus on the past, open old wounds, or rehash what went wrong. Restoring right relationship requires the ability to understand experiences of others, hold ourselves and others accountable for behaviors, and to forgive ourselves and others.

In one parish, further healing, forgiveness, and new life emerged when additional disclosure about misconduct took place fifteen years after the misconduct occurred. Years ago a parish's rector was deposed (removed from ordained ministry pursuant to the canonical disciplinary process) when allegations emerged that he engaged in sexual behavior with a minor.[10] The bishop informed members of the charges and their resolution. Members were aware of the identity of the boy who brought the charges, as his family had spoken to others about the matter. On the whole, members did not believe the adolescent boy; he was perceived to be a "troubled kid." The rector was trusted and loved. The boy and his family left the parish.

---

10. The matter was reported to child protective services as required by state law. These mandatory reporting laws are discussed in chapter 3.

After being removed from the priesthood, the former rector, then working in another setting, sexually abused minors and was arrested, convicted, and served time in prison. Some members began to believe that perhaps there was some truth to what the adolescent boy had alleged; others believed that their former rector was "framed."

Years later, a man from the very first parish where the former rector served told the bishop that he too had been sexually abused by the former rector as an adolescent. Pastoral care and support was offered to this man.[11] This was the first indication that the former rector might have engaged in sexual abuse before he served at the parish from which he was deposed.

The newest allegations brought about additional disclosure in the parish from which the priest was deposed, in part, to prevent members from learning about the latest developments through the press. The bishop met with the vestry and told them that the deposed rector may have sexually abused a minor before ever serving in their parish. The bishop and vestry agreed the best way to proceed was to disclose this information to the entire congregation. A congregational meeting (which followed the protocol set out in chapter 6) was held on a Sunday afternoon. The adolescent boy who made the initial claim that resulted in the priest's deposition was now a young man and chose to attend this meeting. During the meeting many members of the congregation expressed their remorse for not having believed him years earlier and asked his forgiveness.

The process of restoring trust in the wake of misconduct can be long and winding. It requires disclosure of the misconduct in all affected communities. As Christians we are called to disclose misconduct. The adolescent boy, now the young man referred to above, disclosed misconduct. He was courageous; we need to be courageous. Just thinking about disclosing misconduct can give rise to fears and other impediments. It is critical that these impediments and fears be overcome.

---

11. There was no canonical action to be taken as the offender was already deposed from ordained ministry.

Legalities and Liabilities

MISCONDUCT
AND PASTORAL CARE

egal concerns are often one of the first fears expressed by
church members and leaders. To put these concerns in context,
it is important for judicatory and church leaders to understand
secular legal issues that can arise in the wake of misconduct.
Leaders need to know when they are legally required to act (such as
mandatory reporting of suspected abuse and neglect), when to consult an attorney, and how to use advice and counsel from an attorney. An enhanced understanding of legal principles improves leaders'
ability to make informed decisions and explain those decisions to
members of a congregation.

This chapter sets out basic legal information to provide leaders
with a framework for understanding our legal system and common
legal issues. This legal information is *not* specific enough to be used
to make decisions about how to proceed in a specific situation. An
attorney should be engaged to seek legal advice based on the specifics of a given situation.

ECCLESIASTICAL VS. SECULAR LEGAL PROCESSES

Ecclesiastical processes are the processes of the Church, such as ordination, discipline of clergy, placement of clergy in congregations, and

the authority of councils and boards. These processes are framed by canons, the laws of the Church.[1] The secular legal process is governed by laws enacted by Congress or state legislatures within the framework of the U.S. and state Constitutions. These processes are separate from ecclesiastical processes.

In some cases, both secular and ecclesiastical legal processes can come into play. For example, if a priest[2] sexually abuses a child, a number of things will likely occur in the secular legal system: a report is made to state child protective services, a criminal investigation and prosecution commence, and the victim's family could file suit against the congregation and/or the judicatory.[3] In addition, a number of things will likely occur in the ecclesiastical system; a bishop could immediately remove the priest from serving a congregation and commence canonical disciplinary proceedings. While a criminal conviction can result in imprisonment, it cannot remove a member of the clergy from the roles of the church. Only an ecclesiastical process can address the issue of whether a priest continues to be a member of the clergy in good standing.

Secular and ecclesiastical proceedings can move forward simultaneously. In some cases, ecclesiastical processes are put on hold until secular proceedings are resolved. This is particularly true if criminal prosecution is underway. Some terminology used in secular and ecclesiastical proceedings are identical but have different meanings.[4] This can lead to confusion. To provide members of a congregation with clear and timely updates on the status of secular and ecclesiastic

---

1. Generally, secular courts refrain from reviewing cases that focus on how denominations interpret their own canons. The disciplinary canons of the Episcopal Church explicitly state that secular courts do not have authority to interpret or address disputes that arise from these canons (Title IV.19.2 and 3).

2. In the Episcopal Church the disciplinary canons apply to all members of the clergy, which includes deacons, priests, and bishops.

3. Whether a judicatory can be held liable for actions in a congregation depends on the polity of the denomination. This discussion and exploration is beyond the scope of this chapter.

4. For example, a *deposition* in the secular legal system refers to taking sworn testimony of witnesses and other parties before trial as a way of discovering the evidence the other party might present at trial. In the Episcopal Church disciplinary canons, a *deposition* is a sentence imposed on a member of the clergy depriving him or her of the "right to exercise the gifts and spiritual authority of God's word and sacraments conferred at ordination" (Canon IV.2).

proceedings, congregational and judicatory leaders need to have a basic understanding of these processes.

THE SECULAR LEGAL SYSTEM

Scripture urges restraint from use of secular courts to seek redress from Christian sisters and brothers, and yet secular courts are used on a regular basis—victims abused by clergy as children sue as adults, judicatories sue to recover church property taken by former church members who join a different church or denomination, clergy sue when they perceive employment has been terminated unfairly by a congregation or judicatory.

Generally, people resort to secular legal action only after other attempts to resolve a dispute have failed. Using our secular legal system to resolve disputes is monetarily expensive, and is by nature adversarial—that is how our legal system is designed. Using an adversarial system to resolve disputes is likely to enhance alienation in relationships already broken, the antithesis of engaging in God's mission to reconcile all to each other and God. And yet, there are situations that cannot be resolved in any other manner. Sometimes the only way to change an institution is to pursue a matter in secular court.[5]

Many victims of misconduct are not interested in bringing a legal action. They are more interested in healing, being heard and believed, and making sure that no one else is hurt as they were. A timely, thorough, and appropriate pastoral response lets them know they are being heard, taken seriously, and that steps will be taken to prevent future harm to others. This is what we are called to do.

---

5. Take for example the case of *Thurman v. City of Torrington*, 595 F. Supp 1521 (1985). Tracey Thurman sued the Torrington, Connecticut police department on the basis that the police violated her right to equal protection under the law when the police failed to protect her against repeated physical assaults by her husband. The police had been called to her home on numerous occasions for domestic violence complaints. At the time, the law did not require the arrest of alleged perpetrators of family violence. Over time, the police responded to her calls with less urgency even though she had a restraining order. On June 10, 1983, the police arrived twenty-five minutes after Tracey called for help. During this time period, her husband stabbed and beat her. Tracey sustained permanent injuries. In 1986 a federal court awarded her $2.3 million. As a result, the Connecticut legislature passed the Family Violence Prevention and Response Act, which requires police officers to make an arrest whenever there is probable cause that a family violence crime occurred.

This response can also minimize the number of lawsuits filed against a congregation or judicatory. However, not all primary victims will be satisfied with the church's response even if it is thorough, timely, and appropriate. If after investigation a victim's allegations are not fully substantiated, or the sentence imposed is less severe than that which the victim believes is warranted, the victim may be hurt and angry and resort to legal action. These victims believe, on some level, that extracting money from the church will help them heal, prove to others their allegations are true, or force the church to respond in new ways.

Providing Pastoral Care

Parishioners who sue a parish or judicatory for harm inflicted by misconduct remain members of the church; they are still part of the Body of Christ unless they declare otherwise. Being in dispute with the church does not automatically end bonds of Christian fellowship. While it may be counterintuitive, pastoral care and support can still be offered to these primary victims. As litigation is pending, any offers of care and support should be discussed with the attorney representing the church in the matter to ensure that such offers do not waive any rights or claims of the church in the pending litigation. Treating a victim-litigant pastorally does not mean that the church will abandon valid defenses to the victim's legal claims.

Examples of pastoral care that could be offered to a victim-litigant include the following: a priest who could serve as a pastor during this time,[6] a set number of counseling sessions if the victim is in need and without resources,[7] and continuing timely updates as an ecclesiastical disciplinary action proceeds.

---

6. If the offender was the victim's current parish priest and pastor, the victim may now be without a pastor.

7. Bringing a lawsuit alleging one has been victimized is very challenging: the victim's identity is likely known, the victim opens him or herself up to independent evaluations if allegations of physical or emotional harm are made. Moreover, anger of congregants may intensify and be directed at the victim. When offering counseling sessions to any victim, offender, or their family members, it is wise to offer a set predetermined number of sessions; this is not an offer to pay for lifetime therapy. When these expire, an additional specified number of sessions can be offered, if warranted.

OUR SECULAR LEGAL SYSTEM: THE BASICS

There are two broad categories of cases that come before our legal system—criminal cases and civil cases. *Criminal cases* involve prosecution for actions that are defined by law to violate not only individual victim(s), but pose a risk to society as a whole. For example, suppose Joe hits an elderly woman, Mary, over the head and takes her purse. Joe's behavior is an affront to society and potentially risky to other members of society. State authorities criminally prosecute Joe; the name of the case is *State v. Joe*. Joe will be convicted if the state can prove, beyond a reasonable doubt, all the parts of the crimes with which Joe is charged. Joe faces fines and/or time in prison. Criminal cases involve arrests, the police or other law enforcement, and prosecutors, called state's attorneys or district attorneys in some locales—think "Law and Order." In a separate *civil case*, Mary could sue Joe for the value of the money and goods stolen, reimbursement for medical bills, and compensation for her pain and suffering. The name of this case is *Mary v. Joe*. In this case, Joe does not run the risk of going to jail. If Mary wins the civil case, the court will order Joe to pay a certain amount of money to Mary. Mary may have to take additional legal action to actually collect that money from Joe.

Our legal system is composed of state courts and federal courts. State courts, on the whole, interpret and apply state law to settle disputes between residents of a state, or prosecutions for violation of state criminal laws. Federal courts generally interpret and apply federal law, hear cases between residents of different states, or prosecutions for violation of federal criminal laws, such as drug trafficking.

Both the state and federal court systems have trial and appellate courts. A case generally starts in trial court. At trial the judge and jury, if any, hear and see evidence. This can include testimony from witnesses, documents, photographs, and any other types of evidence. At the end of the trial, the judge or jury deliberates to determine whether the prosecutor (in a criminal case) or plaintiff (in a civil case) has proven the necessary facts to establish the legal claim.

Generally, if either party in a *civil* case is unhappy with the trial court's decision and can claim that the unwanted outcome was due to an error in how the trial was conducted, they can appeal the trial court's decision to an appellate court. The appellate court reviews the transcript of the trial proceedings and written legal arguments (called briefs) submitted by attorneys for both parties. The appellate court will hear oral argument from the lawyers. The appellate court does not rehear testimony from witnesses or see other evidence. It makes its decision by reviewing what has already occurred to see if there were any harmful errors in the process.[8] In *criminal* cases, defendants can appeal the trial court's decision if they are convicted. If they are acquitted, the state or federal government is generally not permitted to appeal the decision due to the constitutional bar against double jeopardy.

THE ROLE OF AN ATTORNEY

It is within an attorney-client relationship that an attorney provides specific legal advice pertaining to a client's situation. This *advice* differs from the general legal *information* provided in this book. It is specific legal advice that church leaders take into account when deciding how to proceed in any given matter.

An attorney-client relationship begins when a client hires an attorney; they generally enter into a retainer (a written agreement), which describes the scope of matters for which the attorney will represent the client, and the fee structure. With some limited exceptions, communication between an attorney and client is privileged, which means it is confidential. When a church or judicatory hires a lawyer, not everything every member of the church tells the lawyer falls within this attorney-client privilege. It is important for church leaders to consult with their attorney to know what communications will be privileged.

Typically, the goals of the legal profession are to reduce risks and minimize a client's legal liability. Attorneys can play important roles before and after an event. Beforehand, an attorney's role is to

---

8. The appellate court then rules as to whether the trial court's decision should be upheld, reversed, or modified in some other way.

provide counsel and advice to minimize a client's exposure to risks. Attorneys are trained to try to anticipate all the things that can go wrong. This is why lengthy contracts, spelling out contingencies for all that could go wrong, are sometimes deemed necessary for situations that appear to be simple and straightforward. After an event or incident, the attorney's role is to counsel the client to proceed in a manner that does not expose the client to further risks, and to frame the client's situation in the best light possible when communicating to others and in court.

Choosing an Attorney

When a church faces misconduct, it is wise to engage an attorney who has some experience in the subject matter of the misconduct, such as embezzlement, child sexual abuse, or failure to report suspected abuse as required by law.[9] If a lawsuit is filed naming a church as a defendant, it is likely that the insurance carrier will make provisions for an attorney to defend that suit. Most lawsuits filed against a parish also name the diocese as a defendant based on the assumption that a diocese has legal responsibility for all parishes and more resources to recover in a lawsuit than an individual parish, which may or may not be true. In some situations, the parish and diocese may have different legal arguments and interests. This means that the bishop's attorney, the chancellor, may not be able to provide counsel and advice to a parish.

While the routine legal work of a congregation is often handled by an attorney who is a member of the congregation, in cases of misconduct it is wise to engage a lawyer who is not a member of the congregation. It can be problematic if a member serves as legal counsel to church leaders in the wake of misconduct. The attorney-member will likely need to serve in a professional capacity during much of the time the congregation is processing reactions to misconduct. This diminishes the attorney-member's ability to engage this work on a personal level with other members. The attorney-member may become

---

9. Attorneys may need to familiarize themselves with the canons of the Church. Many attorneys are not familiar with canonical law or the differences in polity among denominations.

alienated if the congregation's leaders treat legal advice as one consideration among many when deciding how to proceed, rather than relying solely on the attorney's suggestions as the blueprint to move forward. Moreover, all members of a congregation, no matter how capable and experienced they are in their profession, can lose professional objectivity when faced with misconduct in their own faith community. When we are emotionally reactive, our logical thought processes and judgment are impaired. For much the same reasons surgeons do not operate on their own children or other loved ones.

MANDATED REPORTING

In the 1970s, states began to pass laws requiring that suspected abuse or neglect of children and elders be reported to designated state authorities. Many states also require the reporting of suspected abuse or neglect of "dependent" adults, or adults with specified disabilities. As mandated reporting laws are state laws, they vary from state to state. Congregational leaders, bishops, priests, and deacons need to know the mandated reporting laws of their state. This information can be found on a state's website, which will likely have specific instructions on who must report, what needs to be reported, and how to report.[10]

State laws vary in specifying who is required to make such reports. In some states, all able adults are deemed to be mandated reporters of suspected abuse. In other states, only those who engage in specified professions are mandated reporters. Teachers, doctors, nurses, childcare providers, and clergy are generally among these professions. In these states where mandated reporters are defined by profession, it is important to remember that *anyone may make a report*, while just those in specified professions are legally obligated to report. Living out our Baptismal Covenant may require us to report suspected abuse or neglect, even if we are not legally obligated to do so.

---

10. It is highly recommended that all training programs to maintain safe and healthy congregations include the reporting obligations based on applicable state law. All ordained and lay leaders need to be aware of these requirements. In some states, departments providing protective services offer live and/or online training regarding legally mandated reporting.

In most states, a mandated reporter must report when they have reason to suspect a person has been, is being, or is at risk of being abused or neglected based on the totality of information known to the reporter.[11] This information can be based on signs the reporter observed or things the reporter has been told by others. The reporter does not have to witness the abuse or neglect.

Most state laws require mandated reporters who have reason to suspect abuse or neglect of a child (usually defined as anyone under eighteen years of age) to report such suspicions to the state's child protective services or the police. Recently there have been an increasing number of criminal prosecutions, in both state and federal courts, for possession of child pornography. Naked pictures of a child or adolescent on a computer, cell phone, or other device should immediately raise concerns. The production of child pornography hurts children; possession of it further exploits them and creates a market for the pornography.

Most states require reports to be made when there is suspected abuse or neglect of an elder or adult who is dependent on another. Some states define "elder" by chronological age, such as "sixty years of age or older." Other states do not use chronological age as a standard but rather focus on the ability of the adult to care for him or herself. Here, if an adult is substantially impaired or is dependent on another person in some way, suspected abuse or neglect must be reported regardless of the adult's chronological age. Again, it is essential to know the reporting requirements of your state.

The consequences of failing to report suspected abuse or neglect vary. Each state's laws set out the penalties that may include fines,

---

11. According to the Book of Common Prayer, any information learned within the sacrament of confession is not to be disclosed under any circumstances: "The secrecy of a confession is morally absolute for the confessor, and must under no circumstances be broken" (BCP, 446). Although confessions may be heard anytime and anywhere, preparation with a penitent before engaging the sacrament is a best practice. Matters learned in the preparation for Reconciliation of a Penitent do not necessarily fall within the "secrecy of confession." Should a mandated reporter learn of abuse or neglect in the midst of the Rite, a priest can withhold pronouncing absolution until the penitent has done what the priest determines is appropriate as a sign of penitence and thanksgiving. In such cases a priest could determine that the penitent and priest together should report the matter to secular authorities. If, however, the penitent refuses, the priest is morally bound to hold the matter in confidence. This moral obligation can conflict with the legal obligation of mandated reporting. Consultation with a bishop is wise anytime a priest is caught in this dilemma.

imprisonment, or both. However, the true cost of failing to report suspected abuse or neglect is the missed opportunity for intervention and potential for continued abuse or neglect of a vulnerable person.

PERSONAL LIABILITY OF CHURCH LEADERS

When a church faces misconduct, a number of fears arise. It is natural for congregational leaders to be concerned about their own personal liability. All churches should have liability insurance for such matters as accidents that might happen on church property, employment claims that could arise, and misconduct. In addition, churches should have director and officers' liability coverage. Leaders do not need to know all the details of insurance coverage, but should be sure that it exists. In some dioceses, coverage is provided through a diocesan insurance program. In other dioceses, parishes purchase insurance coverage on their own.[12]

Generally, director and officers' coverage defends and insures church leaders against personal liability as long as those leaders engage in "due diligence."[13] This means that leaders are expected to apply the generally accepted norms of overseeing and governing the congregation. It is wise for leaders to be aware of the recommended business practices for churches, such as always having two people count the plate offerings, and safe church practices. If diocesan policy and practice requires congregations to conduct criminal record background checks for all adults regularly engaged in ministry with children and youth, it is wise (for many reasons) to be sure this is happening.

LEGAL ADVICE

Generally, attorneys are trained to minimize their client's exposure to financial harm, loss of property, and legal liability. The legal advice given to clients is directed toward these goals and is one important

---

12. There are insurance carriers that specialize in working with churches and are familiar with the unique needs of parishes. The Church Insurance Companies is such a carrier and can be accessed at *www.cpg.org*.

13. Such coverage generally extends to vestry members. It is wise to know how your parish's insurance policy defines "director and officers."

source of information for clients to consider when deciding how to proceed. Lawyers should not decide for clients what clients will do or how they will proceed. This is particularly true for judicatory and congregational leaders. Legal advice to minimize a church's financial and legal liability should be taken into account, and is one of many considerations when deciding how to respond to misconduct. The goal of creating and nurturing communities of Christian fellowship where disciples are formed requires that leaders consider and weigh many factors in addition to legal advice. Some attorneys are able to work with leaders toward these goals, while other attorneys focus solely on reducing or minimizing a church's exposure to legal risk. A process for weighing those risks is set out in the next chapter.

There are a few situations in which church leaders should immediately follow the advice of legal counsel rather than weighing legal advice as one factor to consider. Whenever legal counsel advises reporting to secular authorities the possibility that a crime was committed or someone was abused or neglected, the leadership should not weigh that advice with other considerations. The leadership should immediately follow that advice and make such report. Similarly, if legal counsel advises the retention of documents and information, those documents and information should be kept in a secure location. In some instances, they will need to be retained for years.

It is important for judicatory and congregational leaders to consider legal risks in the wake of misconduct. Some leaders may view potential legal liability as the most important factor to consider in deciding how to move forward. Yet our call is to recreate or restore authenticity and trust among members—not avoid legal liability. It is a trusted Christian community that equips members to engage in God's mission and witness the Good News of Christ in the brokenness of the world, as well as in their faith community.

Even if leaders were to make all decisions with the singular focus of reducing legal liability, that will not eliminate all risk of litigation. Anyone can file a lawsuit against a church, whether or not they have a meritorious claim. It is most important for leaders to remember in the face of fear and threat of legal action, that there are far worse things that can happen to their church than being sued.

4

Weighing the Risks

RESPONDING

Emotions can run high in the immediate wake of misconduct. Both judicatory and congregational leaders can be shocked when allegations of misconduct are first brought forward. In the midst of what can feel like disorienting chaos, judicatory and congregational leaders need to make wise decisions as they seek to care for and support all those impacted by the allegations.

Having a method or process to make decisions can be particularly helpful in times of crisis. When people are anxious, their thinking can become distorted. Risks can feel bigger than they really are, leading to significant fear. The parts of our brain that process fear can override those parts that govern logic and judgment, regardless of our intelligence. When a group of anxious people gather to make decisions together, the conversations can go around in circles, sometimes paralyzing the group, rendering them unable to make reasoned decisions for the good of the congregation.

The decision-making process offered here can help individuals and teams of leaders organize their thoughts so they can make informed decisions. There are six basic steps:

1. Choose a specific action that could be taken.
2. List all the risks of taking that action.

3. For each risk, explore and list possible ways to reduce or eliminate that risk.

4. List all of the risks associated with *not* taking the action identified in Step #1.

5. For each of these risks, explore and list possible ways to reduce or eliminate that risk if the proposed action is not taken.

6. Make a decision.

Here is a simple example of how to use this process. Each morning I park my car in the lot across the street from my office. When I get out of the car and face the building, a four-lane road separates me from the building.

1. Choose a specific action that could be taken

   a. Cross the street to get to my office.

2. List all of the risks of taking that action.

   a. Twisting an ankle or falling as I step off the curb
   b. Getting run over by a car
   c. Dropping something in the middle of the road and not having time to pick it up because of oncoming traffic
   d. Tripping as I step up on the curb on the other side

3. For each risk, explore and list possible ways to reduce or eliminate that risk.

   a. Look down as I step off the curb and step carefully.
   b. Look both ways before I start to cross the street.
   c. Pack my things carefully and securely.
   d. Look down as I step up on the curb on the other side.

4. List all of the risks associated with *not* taking that action identified in Step #1 (which in this case is not crossing the street and staying in the parking lot).

   a. Loss of opportunities to collaborate with my colleagues face to face
   b. Inability to work at my desk

    c. Lack of physical presence for pastoral conversations

    d. Loss of employment is a long-term risk.

5. For each of these risks, explore and list possible ways to reduce or eliminate that risk if the proposed action is not taken.

    a. Enhance capacity to participate in virtual meetings.

    b. Set up an extensive home office with all of the resources and paper files that are available to me in my employer's workspace.

    c. Keep in touch with staff members by email and text.

    d. Try to have pastoral intervention conversations by phone or Skype.

    e. Find a job with parking on the same side of the street as the office.

6. Make a decision. I look both ways, carefully step off the curb, carry my securely packed bags, swiftly walk across the street, and carefully step up on the curb on the other side.

Another way to view this decision-making process is to use a chart such as that in the figure "Decision-Making Process" overleaf.

While this example might seem trivial, it demonstrates a process that can support church leaders when faced with decisions about matters that are not trivial, but quite serious. Often after a decision has been made, a member of a leadership team will wonder aloud, "Did we consider . . . ?" "What if . . . ?" "So and so really isn't going to like this." Leaders can remind themselves and each other of the basis for their decisions if they fully explore the risks and ways to reduce or eliminate risks. This process can help equip leaders to explain the basis of their decisions to each other and members of the congregation.

A CASE STUDY

Imagine a church where the long-tenured, married, soon-to-retire rector begins a sexualized relationship with a recently widowed woman in the parish. The wardens and other members can see what is going on. The wardens ask the rector to end the

DECISION-MAKING PROCESS:
WEIGHING THE RISKS OF ACTING AND NOT ACTING

STEP 1: Choose a specific action: Crossing the street to get to work

STEP 2: List risks of taking action

1. Twisting an ankle or falling as I step off the curb
2. Getting run over by a car
3. Dropping something in the middle of the road and not having time to pick it up because of oncoming traffic
4. Tripping as I step up on the curb on the other side

STEP 3: List ways to reduce or eliminate risks

1. Look down as I step off the curb, and step carefully
2. Look both ways before I start to cross the street
3. Pack my things carefully and securely
4. Look down as I step up on the curb on the other side

STEP 4: List risks of *not* taking action: (not crossing the street)

1. Loss of opportunities to collaborate with my colleagues face-to-face
2. Inability to work at my desk
3. Lack of physical presence for pastoral conversations
4. Loss of employment is a long-term risk

STEP 5: List ways to reduce or eliminate risks

1. Enhance capacity to participate in virtual meetings
2. Set up an extensive home office with all of the resources and paper files that are available to me in my employer's workspace
3. Keep in touch with staff members by email and text
4. Try to have pastoral conversations by phone or Skype
5. Find a job with parking on the same side of the street as the office

STEP 6: Decide: Carefully cross the street

relationship. The rector refuses. The wardens and rector decide together that to resolve this problem the rector will retire a bit sooner than originally planned and nothing will be said about the sexualized relationship. The rector's retirement is announced and a party is planned. A member of the congregation, who witnessed misconduct in her former church, knows this is wrong. She raises her concerns with members of the vestry. The vestry tells her not to discuss this matter with others and to let the rector retire. She reports her concerns to the bishop who immediately recognizes that an intervention is needed. Judiciary staff members work with congregational leaders to explore their fears (risks) and ways to minimize those risks. In essence, the judiciary staff led the congregation's leaders through the process of weighing risks.

DECISION-MAKING PROCESS: WEIGHING THE RISKS OF ACTING AND NOT ACTING

STEP 1: Choose a specific action:
Telling the congregation that the rector is on leave because he engaged in a sexual relationship with an adult member of the parish

STEP 2: List risks of taking action

1. Rector's wife will be embarrassed.
2. Youth will know what happened.
3. We will get sued for defamation, libel, and slander.
4. This will put a damper on the retirement party.
5. Members will be angry at the woman who told the judiciary.
6. Pledging will go down because people love the rector.

STEP 3: List ways to reduce or eliminate risks

1. She already knows her husband is unfaithful; judiciary staff will offer support, and meet with her before any disclosure to the congregation to share what will be disclosed.
2. Youth already know more than many adult members. Provide a separate meeting for youth so they can process misconduct as a community of youth.

Continued

DECISION-MAKING PROCESS *Continued*

STEP 2:

7. Members will be angry at the woman engaged in the relationship with the rector. She is recently widowed and needs her community of support.

STEP 3:

3. Carefully craft the disclosure statement to ensure clarity of allegations versus facts.[1]

4. True. Education about dynamics of misconduct and the value of Christian fellowship in a community of truth-tellers can ease this disappointment.

5. Her name will not be disclosed, yet it is possible that members will figure out who reported this matter. The bishop can indicate the church "became aware of the rector's behavior" without indicating anyone who reported to the judicatory. She will receive care and support at each step of the process, members will be educated on why it is important to report such matters, judicatory will express gratitude for her courage, if necessary.

6. It might, and such a decrease in pledges can be minimized by focusing on the health of the congregation and the importance of this community to members, rather than the importance of the ordained leader.

7. Her name will not be disclosed. Members may know or figure out her identity. Education on power dynamics in ministerial relationships will help members understand that the rector is responsible to maintain professional boundaries.

Continued

---

1. Speaking the truth about a situation does not create liability for harming another's reputation. In this case, if the rector's reputation is harmed, it is because he engaged in misconduct at the end of a long career.

DECISION-MAKING PROCESS *Continued*

STEP 4: List risks of not taking action: (This is the list from chapter 2.)

1. Displaced residual anger, sadness, and distrust can continue for years.
2. Unacceptable behavior is condoned by silence.
3. Trust is not restored and continues to erode.
4. Energy is spent on ignoring and hiding the truth rather than engaging mission and ministry.
5. Formation of disciples is curtailed. Members become reluctant to bring their own brokenness to the community, as the community does not have the capacity to speak of the brokenness within itself.
6. Primary victims are blamed because of the lack of understanding of the power dynamics at play.
7. Primary victims may feel unheard.
8. Others are not encouraged to recognize their victimization (in the church or in other settings) and heal from such misconduct.
9. The congregation is denied an opportunity to be educated and establish healthy boundaries and systems of checks and accountability.
10. Some members know what is going on; some know something is going on, but do not have accurate information. This creates a power differential between those with knowledge and those without.

STEP 5: List ways to reduce or eliminate risks

1. There is virtually no way to reduce or eliminate these risks without telling members about the misconduct.

STEP 6: Decide: Will disclose to congregation that the rector is on leave because he engaged in a sexual relationship with an adult member of the parish

The decision to disclose misconduct can be better understood by leaders who have completed the process of weighing the risks of disclosing and not disclosing. This process could be further repeated to address all the fears and risks judicatory and congregational leaders encounter in the wake of misconduct. Identifying the risks in Step #2 and how to reduce them in Step #3 helps to frame and create a blueprint for how to move forward. This process can also be useful whenever a decision involves complex issues, large amounts of data, or is emotionally charged. A blank chart to support this decision-making process of weighing the risks of acting and not acting is included in Appendix A.

We will next explore the principles of crafting a statement to disclose misconduct to members of a congregation. This process of weighing risks can be used to determine the content of the disclosure statement.

The Disclosure Statement
One Voice

rafting a disclosure statement about misconduct is important; it contains the information that will be shared with all
members of a congregation and beyond. It is through the
sharing of this statement that members receive accurate,
timely information. This is one of the first steps toward rebuilding
trust among members of a congregation.

In most situations involving *clergy* misconduct, a bishop or
judicatory staff member shares a disclosure statement with wardens, then vestry members, then staff, and then all members of a
congregation. This is how a bishop informs a congregation of misconduct and any action taken pursuant to the denomination's disciplinary process. If misconduct involves a *lay* leader, the disclosure
statement may be crafted and read by the ordained leadership of
that church.

Statements for the press are different from disclosure statements
for a congregation. Generally, there is more specific information
shared with a congregation than with the media. A fuller discussion
regarding statements for the press is included later in this chapter.
The entire process of sharing disclosure statements and providing
opportunities for members to process, ask questions, and share concerns is reviewed in chapter 6.

Generally, any time allegations of misconduct are brought forward and/or disciplinary action is commenced, it is appropriate

to consider informing a congregation that questions have been raised regarding the propriety of a leader's behavior.[1] Since the goal of creating a disclosure statement is to provide members with accurate and timely information, more than one disclosure statement will likely be needed. As a matter unfolds, more facts will become known in the normal course of the process or through a formal investigation. In addition, it is important for members to be updated as a matter proceeds through different stages of the disciplinary process and the final resolution. Assurance that members will receive timely updates helps to reduce rumors and anxiety.

CRAFTING A DISCLOSURE STATEMENT

The time and energy it takes to craft a disclosure statement is well spent. First, it necessitates the person or team drafting the statement to become quite clear as to what will be shared and the specific language to be used. Having intentionally determined what will be shared and what will not be shared means there is less chance of mistakenly sharing something that should be held in confidence. Moreover, having a single statement to share with a congregation increases the likelihood that every member will hear the same information. The statement ensures uniformity of message regardless of who is sharing the statement. This is particularly important if a bishop and other staff members are collaborating to respond to misconduct.

There are seven basic principles that guide the crafting of a disclosure statement.

Appendix B contains a worksheet to assist in applying these principles. Appendix C contains examples of disclosure statements used in a variety of circumstances.

---

1. The decision to disclose allegations to a congregation is dependent upon the significance and degree of abuse of power asserted in the allegations. While transparency and openness can be essential, if allegations consist of one challenging interaction with one parishioner, it may benefit both parties to focus on reconciliation as each takes responsibility for their contribution to the challenging interaction and not disclose this to the congregation.

1. Start with the truth.

Instead of spending time and energy wondering about what to share with a congregation, just start with the truth. Start with the basic facts of the (alleged) misconduct that are known to date. Add to that the steps taken by judicatory or congregational leaders to respond.

A disclosure statement should include the following essential information: the nature of the misconduct, when the misconduct occurred, when judicatory/church leaders first learned of the misconduct, how judicatory/church leaders have responded, assurance that all those impacted are being offered care and support, any involvement of secular courts, and whether any reports were made to secular authorities pursuant to mandated reporting laws.

> The Episcopal Church disciplinary canons require bishops to provide an appropriate pastoral response to all affected by alleged misconduct including the affected community. The canons repeatedly authorize bishops to disclose information related to misconduct "as the bishop deems pastorally appropriate."[2]

2. Balance the need for transparency with confidentiality.

Members need to know what has happened, is currently happening, and what will likely happen in the future. This does not include personal information about individuals directly involved or impacted by the misconduct. For example, if allegations are pending against a priest and the bishop determines a psychological or psychiatric evaluation would be helpful in discerning next steps, the bishop would not necessarily share this with the members of the congregation. What the bishop might share is, "I am consulting with professional resources as we move forward in the process." Similarly, if a member of the cleric's family is taking advantage of therapeutic counseling paid for by the judicatory, it is not appropriate to include that fact in

---

2. See Title IV.7.9, 8.3, and 14.13. For the canons pertaining to confidential communication and privileged communication, see Title IV.19.26 and 19.27, respectively.

the disclosure statement. What can be included is, "We are working with all individuals directly impacted, including the families of those individuals, to offer care and support at this challenging time."

> The Episcopal Church canons require bishops to consider the privacy interests and pastoral needs of all affected when providing an appropriate pastoral response to misconduct.[3]

3. Use information from public records if possible.

Anyone can get access to public records, including the press. Information contained in public records is not confidential. Public records include arrest reports, police reports, and most documents filed in secular civil court.

If a church leader is sued in civil court, the allegations in the complaint are often available to the public, as are any responses to those allegations filed by the leader. If a former rector is sued for failing to repay a loan from a member of a congregation, for violating confidences of a parishioner, or having sexual contact with a minor, members of the congregation benefit from learning about this within their community of faith.

When allegations of misconduct become known by virtue of an arrest, often the essential facts (or allegations) of the matter are contained in the arrest and police reports. In such case a disclosure statement might read, "On Thursday of last week, Rector X was arrested at his home for allegedly physically assaulting his spouse" or whatever the case may be, such as possession of narcotics or child pornography. The statement discloses the essence of what is contained in the arrest report. While it is true that many criminal charges are reduced in severity as a criminal prosecution progresses, at this point the disclosure statement should indicate the current charge(s). To indicate otherwise would be to speculate as to what might happen, and it is best to avoid speculation in disclosure statements.

---

3. Title IV.8.4.

It is better for members of a congregation to learn about misconduct from the bishop or parish leaders rather than the press. Feelings of betrayal are compounded when members learn their rector violated the trust of their community on the six o'clock news, rather than from the judicatory or parish leaders. If the press receives and reports public information before church leaders are aware of it, then the leadership can quickly arrange for a meeting of the congregation as described in the next chapter and craft a disclosure statement for that meeting.

4. Avoid disclosing the identity of primary victim(s).

It is not the place of church leadership to disclose the identity of primary victims. Leaders should disclose the nature and timeframe of misconduct—this is the church's story. The primary victim's story does not belong to the church—it is not the church's to tell. It is up to the primary victim if he or she wants to tell the story. The primary victim has already been violated. It is the church's responsibly to respond to the misconduct, provide members with information and support to build a trusting, authentic community, and not to further violate the victim.[4]

While not disclosing the identity of a primary victim, it is essential that disclosure statements include whether the primary victim is a member (or was a member) of the congregation. There is a significant difference between a married rector having a sexualized relationship with an adult who is not affiliated with the congregation, and one who is member of the congregation. Both are a betrayal of members' trust, yet the power dynamics and the impact on the congregation can be quite different.

---

4. If a primary victim wants to disclose his or her identity, he or she should make this determination only after being informed of the typical reactions of members when they learn of congregational misconduct. A victim motivated to disclose their identity for the purpose of receiving care and support from members might best be counseled to accept care and support from other sources. However, if a victim wants to disclose his or her identity, it can be done in collaboration with the judicatory. In some situations, knowing the identity of the primary victim can help members of a congregation move forward more readily as they have a greater degree of accurate information. Under no circumstances should a primary victim be pressured to disclose their identity.

Some primary victims are fearful that any disclosure to the congregation will lead to the discovery of their identity. While a valid concern, a victim's fear and concerns do not override the need to care for the community by providing timely accurate information. Navigating these competing needs requires the utmost care. A fuller discussion of special considerations regarding care and support of primary victims is included in chapter 11.

5. Identify whether victims are minors or adults in cases involving sexual misconduct.

If this is not made clear to members, they may incorrectly assume the worst. If a statement only discloses "There are allegations that your rector has engaged in sexual misconduct with a member of the congregation," fear will set in among members that the misconduct involved minors. For many members their worst fear, perhaps sparked by news reports from the Roman Catholic Church, is that a child has been sexually abused. If the allegation involves sexual abuse of a child, then the disclosure statement needs to so indicate. If on the other hand the rector had a sexualized relationship with an adult member of the congregation, the statement needs to indicate this.

6. Be brief.

The disclosure statement should be no longer than a few sentences—a paragraph at most. When we are stressed, our minds can process only limited amounts of information.[5] You don't want to include so much detail about the first point that members are unable to attend to the following essential points. Remember, a key reason to disclose misconduct is so that all members receive the same accurate, timely information. The goal is to present the information in a way that is accessible to as many members as possible.

---

5. You may have experienced this if you have ever received a serious diagnosis from a doctor. In those moments, even the most logical, intelligent people report being unable to comprehend all the information presented and ask all the necessary questions to make informed decisions.

For example, a bishop's disclosure statement might read, in part, "I learned of these allegations on Monday and I met with your rector on Tuesday to inform her that effective immediately, she was on administrative leave while the disciplinary process proceeds." The statement does not include details of the disciplinary process, any rights the rector might have to contest the imposition of administrative leave, or what the next steps in the disciplinary process might be. It also does not include details about the administrative leave, whether it is paid or unpaid, who will serve the congregation during the leave, and so forth. A disclosure statement is read to members in the context of a congregational meeting, which affords members an opportunity to ask questions and express concerns and feelings. The details can be given in response to questions. Having previously done the work to determine what information is appropriate to share and what is appropriately held in confidence will make responding to questions easier.

7. Have legal counsel review the content of the statement.

There may be ways to word a disclosure statement that reduces exposure to legal liability while still effectively communicating the truth. For this reason it is important to have counsel review it prior to sharing it with others.

Working with the Media

A common concern expressed by leaders and members of congregations is the fear that the press will pick up the story about misconduct. Interestingly, the most commonly expressed fear is that the local weekly or daily publication will run the story and everyone at the grocery store will know what's happening. Ideally a statement for the press is ready before inquiries from the press begin, and guidance is provided to members about how to respond if the press contacts them. This guidance is an aspect of caring, supporting, and providing a pastoral response to all members of a parish.

Statements for media and press generally include less detail than the disclosure statement for members of a congregation, and yet every disclosure statement for congregations should be written so that if it is reprinted in a newspaper, on a website, or via social media, nothing inappropriate would be disclosed. Statements for the press can include: an acknowledgment of the allegations pending, a general regret for any harm caused by this type of misconduct globally, acknowledgment of reports made to secular authorities or cooperation with secular authorities as the matter is investigated, and affirmation of prayers for all involved.

A press statement regarding allegations of child sex abuse by a lay leader might read, "The church community is saddened by the allegations that a child has been harmed. Church leaders are cooperating with the authorities and look forward to the findings of their investigation. We pray for healing and wholeness for all children who have been abused." While this statement does not disclose a lot of specific information, it is far better than issuing a statement that says, "No comment." Appendix D contains examples of press statements used in a variety of circumstances.

In some cases, the judicatory and the congregation will have separate statements for the press. It is helpful if these statements are shared among these leaders before they are shared with the media. In other cases, the judicatory will create a statement for the press and the congregation's leaders will decide to refer all inquiries from the press to the spokesperson for the judicatory. In the midst of providing a pastoral response to all affected by misconduct, our initial focus should be on the individuals directly impacted and the congregation. The drafting of a statement for the press is important, but shouldn't detract energy and resources from caring for the individuals and community most impacted.

Whenever there is any type of crisis (the realization that misconduct may have occurred is a time of crisis for any congregation), it is important to appoint one person to be a spokesperson. All leaders and members need to know who their spokesperson is. All inquiries from the press can be referred to this person, who will read the prepared statement for the press. It is usually wise for the spokesperson to just read the statement and indicate that the statement is all they have to say.

A church's leaders and members should be informed that they are under no obligation to speak to a member of the press if they do not want to. Often, members are relieved to hear this and glad that there is a spokesperson to speak on behalf of their parish.[6] It is helpful if members of the congregation know the content of the statement for the press before it is released. This helps avoid any surprises and demonstrates that the leadership is open and transparent. This is critical as members grapple with the secrets of misconduct coming to light. It can also be helpful to remind members that misconduct seems newsworthy because of the great impact it has on their lives and their congregation; however, it may not be the most newsworthy matter to the press. There are situations one would expect the press to report and they do not.

Deciding when to give a statement to the press can be difficult. It is good for church leadership to be timely and forthright and have their statement included in the initial reporting of a matter. Yet ideally, members should hear what is happening in their congregation before the press and the rest of the world hear it. This requires that statements be given to the press only after the disclosure statement has been shared with members at a congregational meeting, which is not always possible.

As Christians we are called to bring secrets into the light. Disclosing the secrets of misconduct is necessary to restore trust after misconduct. Determining what is disclosed about misconduct is informed by the competing needs of transparency and the confidential nature of pastoral concerns and personal information. The seven principles of crafting a disclosure statement can guide judicatories and church leaders through this process. Deciding what will be disclosed is an important step in the process of restoring trust in the wake of misconduct.

---

6. Under no circumstances should members be told that they cannot, or are prohibited from, speaking to the press. It is the member's choice. Judicatory and church leaders can help members make informed choices by educating them about the designation of a spokesperson for the congregation and content of the prepared statement for the media.

6

The Disclosure Process
THE CONGREGATION

Disclosing misconduct to members of a congregation entails more than crafting and sharing a disclosure statement; it requires creating opportunities for leaders and members to hear the content of the statement in settings that invite their questions and concerns. A disclosure meeting needs to be safe for all members to voice the diversity of their reactions, knowing that all reactions are honored. Members need to know that the differences in the ways they react to misconduct will not destroy their community. They need to experience and know how to support each other in these differences. This can lead to a deeper level of authenticity among members and enhance the experience of Christian fellowship.

This disclosure process is offered as a way to inform and care for all those impacted by misconduct. The suggestions presented have been tried, modified, and repeatedly used with a variety of congregations facing misconduct.[1] Ideally each step in this process would be taken every time an allegation of misconduct is made, but this is not always possible. Awareness of an ideal process can help inform the process that is possible.

---

1. In addition, this process has been modified and used with congregations and smaller communities within a church that need to engage in other challenging conversations, such as whether a church is financially viable, the changing role of the church in the twenty-first century, and the need for long-serving, entrenched lay leaders to step aside to allow new leaders to emerge and assume authority.

Responding to misconduct cannot be scheduled ahead of time. It is impossible to know when a primary victim will decide the time is right for him or her to tell church authorities about abuse, or when police will determine there is enough evidence to make an arrest. Timing is a critical element of responding to misconduct, often requiring that other important matters be rescheduled. While an ideal response may be impossible, the best possible response given the circumstances should be offered.

MISCONDUCT BY LAY VS. ORDAINED LEADERS

In the Episcopal Church, bishops are responsible for the discipline of clergy and for providing an appropriate pastoral response for all impacted by misconduct. The process to disclose misconduct in congregations, as described here, is a process to respond to misconduct by an ordained leader. It assumes an active role for the bishop and judicatory staff. The process can be readily modified for use in cases of lay misconduct. Rather than the bishop, the rector is responsible for responding to lay misconduct in a parish. Rectors, wardens, and vestries generally have very limited experience in responding to lay misconduct in their parish. They usually welcome and are grateful for assistance and support from judicatory staff and bishops with such responses.

THE FACILITATORS

Ideally, congregational disclosure meetings are facilitated by teams of two, with the bishop serving as one member, at least for the initial meeting to disclose clergy misconduct.[2] It is best for the teams to be balanced for gender, and composed of a lay person and an ordained person who are not members of the congregation. Parish leaders, who may be gifted facilitators, should have the opportunity to fully participate in the healing process as members of the congregation

---

2. While it is desirable for the bishop to be present throughout the process as a congregation works to restore trust, this is not always possible. This requires striking a balance between the need to keep the process moving forward and the desire to have the bishop present.

without having to carry the responsibility of guiding the disclosure meeting. Like all members, they need an opportunity to move toward reconciliation in their own relationships with others. Furthermore, if the disclosure meeting appears to be driven by any members of the congregation, the integrity of the process can be questioned if those members appear to have taken sides in the misconduct, or have an interest in how the misconduct is resolved.[3]

Facilitators need to be firmly grounded in their faith and self-differentiated. Facilitators may well be the recipients of members' displaced anger and other negative emotions during parish conversations about misconduct. If facilitators are reactive or defensive, the effectiveness of the process is greatly diminished. Facilitators need to be non-anxious; they need to be a peaceful, grounded presence in the midst of great anxiety. In addition, they should be articulate in, and have a deep appreciation of, the effects of congregational misconduct.

THE PRESENCE OF PRIMARY VICTIMS

Whether a primary victim attends the disclosure meeting is a decision that needs to be made by the victim.[4] The role of the bishop and judicatory staff is to provide the victim with information so the victim can make an informed decision. The victim's decision should be based on what will best meet his or her individual needs as he or she moves toward healing and wholeness. In making this decision, victims may benefit from encouragement to focus on their own needs rather than those of the congregation.

Factors that motivate a victim to attend include the desire to hear exactly what is shared by the bishop and/or judicatory staff, to witness how members respond to the disclosure of misconduct, to be part of the congregation as it moves through this process, and the perceived need to be in attendance so that other members do not

---

3. Generally, it is advisable for all difficult conversations in congregations to be facilitated by someone who is not a member of that congregation.

4. This discussion pertains to adults who are currently members of the congregation in which the misconduct occurred. The misconduct may have been relatively recent, or may have occurred decades ago when the victim was a child.

infer the identity of the victim by the victim's absence from the meeting (assuming the victim does not want their identity disclosed). In making this decision, victims benefit from knowing how the disclosure meeting will be structured, content of the disclosure statement, identity of facilitators, the role of lay leaders, and how members might react to the disclosure. A victim should be prepared that members may react angrily toward him or her.

Victims who choose to attend and wish to keep their identity confidential cannot receive special support from the facilitators at the meeting—this would risk disclosure of their identity. These victims need other sources of support on which they can rely during and immediately after the meeting. Those who choose not to attend should receive an oral report from a judicatory leader within hours of the meeting's conclusion.

In my experience, victims who want to keep their identity confidential and continue as a member in a congregation where they were victimized, find attending the disclosure meeting very difficult. And yet, each has reported benefits from attending. The benefits from attending include: learning that some members are relieved that the victim reported the misconduct; knowing which members are hostile toward the victim; hearing firsthand how other members are impacted (as secondary victims) by the misconduct; and, perhaps most importantly, hearing on a deeper level that ordained leaders are always responsible for maintaining professional boundaries, regardless of circumstance—in other words, hearing that the victim did not cause the misconduct. Attending the meeting is not the right decision for every victim. All victims should be supported in their decision, whether or not they decide to attend.

THE PRESENCE OF ALLEGED OFFENDERS

The presence of an alleged offender at a disclosure meeting can inhibit members' ability to openly ask the hard questions and express varying opinions and reactions. Moreover, members may focus on the needs of the alleged offender rather than focusing on their own needs. If an *ordained* offender no longer serves the congregation, or has been put on leave by the bishop as a result of the allegations, the offender should most definitely not be present at the disclosure meeting. If, however, there is a need to disclose alleged misconduct to a congregation while the alleged offender is still serving the congregation, the question of their presence is much more complicated.[5] Ordained leaders need to know about the life of the community they serve and generally need to be present for such a disclosure meeting.

Clergy serving a congregation while facing allegations of misconduct need to be well supported. This is a time of heightened anxiety, which impairs their ability to make thoughtful decisions and increases the probability of reactive behavior. In such cases, clergy are likely to process their own responses to the misconduct with members of the congregation rather than outside resources. Some members will closely watch the cleric in anticipation of his or her next misstep. This is a challenging situation for all involved. For a discussion of ways to support those who offend or are alleged to have offended, see chapter 11.

When the alleged offender is a lay leader, he or she can be asked not to attend a disclosure meeting. The considerations that justify the presence of an ordained offender at a disclosure meeting do not apply equally to a lay leader. It is generally wise to direct a lay offender not to attend a disclosure meeting.

PLANNING THE DISCLOSURE

As soon as the bishop recognizes that there is information regarding clergy misconduct to disclose, he or she and/or the judicatory staff meet with the wardens. This could be soon after allegations are raised if the bishop discerns the need to limit the cleric's ministry in any way. This meeting is best done face-to-face, but can be done via conference call or Skype. The three goals of this conversation are (1) to inform the wardens of the allegations/misconduct, (2) to set a

---

5. There is no doubt that disclosing misconduct to a congregation in which the offender/ alleged offender continues to serve can undermine the cleric's authority, ability to lead, and trust of members. Frequently, however, the trust is already considerably eroded and undermined by the cleric's actions (or perceived actions) that spawned the allegations or evidence of misconduct.

time for the bishop and judicatory staff to meet with the vestry (generally, the wardens are asked to invite vestry members to this meeting), and (3) to assure the wardens that they and the congregation will be supported as they move through this challenging time.

The vestry is the next community within the congregation that should learn of the misconduct. This allows vestry members to begin to process their personal reactions to the misconduct so they can better function as leaders, focusing on the good of the whole, when all members learn of the misconduct. The process to disclose to the vestry is the same process that will be used to disclose to the congregation.

After learning of the misconduct, the vestry provides input for the congregational disclosure meeting by working with the bishop and/or judicatory staff to determine (1) when the disclosure meeting for all members will occur; (2) the logistics of that meeting—room setup, microphone, coffee, and other hospitality measures; (3) the timing and method of inviting members to this meeting; (4) whether disclosure to parish staff should occur immediately before the disclosure to members; and (5) whether there are any individuals who may be uniquely impacted by this news and best cared for by learning about the misconduct in a smaller group. There may not be anyone in this category, but it could include extended family members of the cleric. If there are individuals in this group, this disclosure conversation is best held within hours of the congregational disclosure meeting.

Whether staff members should learn of the misconduct separately from the members of the congregation is determined on a case-by-case basis. In part, this depends on the size of the staff. Staff may be impacted in specific ways and have questions regarding supervision and day-to-day operations. If there is a separate disclosure meeting for staff, it should immediately precede the congregational meeting. Ideally wardens or a team of vestry members are present for this meeting as a way of providing ongoing support to staff members.

Disclosure meetings with staff and individuals uniquely impacted can be less formal than the vestry and congregational disclosure meetings due to the smaller size of these groups. However, it is important for the same disclosure statement and educational information to be shared. One way of doing this is by explaining what will happen in the congregational disclosure meeting. All of the key points can be presented and discussed in that explanatory overview.

The next community within the congregation that needs to learn of the misconduct is that of the adult members of the congregation. This is likely the largest group that will gather for a disclosure meeting. Typically, parents find it helpful to attend this meeting before deciding how their children and youth should learn of the misconduct. It is best left to parents to decide if youth will attend the congregational disclosure meeting.

After the congregational disclosure meeting, parents and youth ministers can inform the process of how children and youth will learn about the misconduct and best be supported. Generally, this will entail a number of conversations with different developmental age groupings. It is wise to consult with a child educator and/or child psychologist to determine the level of detail to disclose and other age-appropriate considerations. Individuals who have experience in working with children and youth best lead these conversations; this may or may not be the bishop or judicatory staff.

MANAGING INFORMATION

After misconduct is disclosed to the wardens and vestry, they are asked to hold the matter in confidence until it is shared with the entire congregation. This helps ensure that all members hear the same information at the same time. It can reduce speculation and rumors, minimizing the likelihood that members will hear incomplete or inaccurate information that could lead some to jump to conclusions, take a position on the matter, or draw a line in the sand. Such reactions make the work of helping members support each other while honoring their differences even more challenging.

The reason that the timing of these initial disclosure meetings is so critical is, in part, to reduce the amount of time (and burden) wardens, vestry, and staff will have of holding the information in confidence. Ideally, the staff disclosure meeting will end as the congregational disclosure meeting is about to begin.

SETTING THE TIME

Set aside at least two hours for a congregational disclosure meeting. In a large congregation, even more time may be needed to ensure there is adequate time for people to share if they so choose. The time and day of the meeting should be scheduled to fit the needs of the congregation as well as the bishop's schedule.

The congregational meeting should be scheduled so that all members feel free to participate or not. It is best if it is not held immediately before, during or after, worship. This prevents the focus of worship from being shifted to the misconduct, and truly provides members with a choice as to whether they attend the disclosure meeting. Members may feel pressured to attend the meeting if it begins right after worship, requiring them to visibly excuse themselves from the meeting or walk through the space where the meeting is commencing. For some members, misconduct brings up other instances of betrayal or victimization in their lives. It may be better for theses members to process the misconduct at another time in another setting. The decision of whether to attend a congregational disclosure meeting is best made by each member.

INVITING MEMBERS

The congregational disclosure meeting should be scheduled for as soon as possible after the disclosure to vestry members. It is important that parish leaders be prepared to send out an invitation using all communication methods available. This usually includes an email blast, electronic newsletter, snail mail, worship bulletin, social media, and reading the invitation at announcement time during worship. When drafting written communications regarding misconduct, assume that members of the press will gain access to them.

The content of the invitation should give enough information so that members know what this meeting is about, but not disclose information that hasn't already been disclosed.[6] If there has been

---

6. It is undesirable for members to learn about misconduct in isolation from the community, as there is no opportunity for leaders to immediately respond to concerns or provide care and support.

a public event, such as an arrest, the invitation can reference that event. An invitation to a congregational disclosure meeting could read as follows:

> Your wardens, vestry, and Bishop X invite all adult members of ABC Church to attend an important meeting in the life of our congregation on [date] and [time] in ABC's parish hall. Bishop X has information to share regarding the leadership of our parish. This will be a time for us to gather together, understand the challenges we are facing, and explore ways to minister to each other as we move forward. Please make every effort to attend.

Members will immediately know that something is afoot since the bishop is making an unscheduled visit to the parish. Members are likely to ask questions of the wardens and vestry. It is wise for leaders to listen and hear the concerns of members but take care not to share any confidential information. Leaders can ask members to refrain from speculating and urge them to attend the congregational disclosure meeting.

Additional sample invitations that have been used in a variety of situations are included in Appendix E.

Room Arrangement

Generally, meeting in a parish hall is preferable to meeting in worship space. It usually provides greater flexibility of setup. If there isn't an adequate parish hall or large community room, the congregational meeting can be held in the nave, but be aware that some congregations find it difficult to talk about misconduct in their worship space. Parish leaders can provide guidance on this.

The congregation may have a standard way of gathering for meetings: theater style, sitting around one table (for smaller congregations), or sitting at multiple tables for discussion (for larger congregations). If there is some sort of room setup that the congregation is familiar with, try to honor that.

If twenty-five or fewer members are expected to attend the disclosure meeting, sitting in a circle where members can all see each other is ideal. It is important to try to incorporate all members in one circle so that no individual is sitting outside the circle. An option for larger groups is to set up rows of chairs arranged in a "U" shape so that members can see each other rather than all facing the front of the room. For very large groups, consider setting up tables with chairs around them so that members can engage in table conversations. For most congregational disclosure meetings, it is best to keep everyone engaged together in one large group conversation. However, with very large groups it may be necessary to allow people to express their concerns in small groups and then share them with the full group.[7]

It is important for everyone to be able to hear clearly what is shared. Determine whether a microphone system will be needed. If so, identify someone who has experience using the sound amplification system that will set it up beforehand and operate it during the meeting.

PUBLIC OR PRIVATE?

The congregational meeting is *not* open to the general public. At the beginning of the meeting, the bishop or another facilitator will inquire whether anyone present is a member of the press or otherwise not a member of the congregation. Any such individuals are politely invited to leave so as to allow the congregation to have conversation as a community of faith. Indicate that anyone who is a member of the congregation as well as a member of the press is asked to be present in their capacity as a member of the congregation. Emphasize that this is not a "secret" meeting, but rather a gathering of the congregation, as a means of providing care and support to its members.

Generally, leaders will know whether there are nonmembers present. Even if everyone present is a member, it is advisable to explain that the meeting is not open to the public or the press, as a

---

7. A variation successfully used by some dioceses is to bring in members of a *Pastoral Response Team* to serve as facilitators at each table. Members of the team are knowledgeable in how misconduct impacts a congregation and its members, and are gifted facilitators who are able to be non-anxious and pastoral in the midst of crisis. These team members may be lay or ordained. Generally, they serve on a volunteer basis.

way to set the tone for the congregation's time together. If the misconduct is a high-profile matter, you may want to consider providing the press with a press statement *after* the congregational meeting.

AN OUTLINE OF A CONGREGATIONAL DISCLOSURE MEETING

The structure of a congregational disclosure meeting includes the following:

1. Opening prayer

The bishop, congregational leader, or a facilitator opens the meeting with prayer. It is preferable not to include prayers for matters directly related to the misconduct. No matter how carefully language is chosen, there is a risk that some members will interpret the prayer as "taking sides" in the matter.

2. Introductory matters

There are four areas encompassed in introductory matters:

a. Welcome members of the congregation and thank them for coming to this important gathering. Explain that the meeting is an opportunity for members to learn accurate information about a difficult situation, and have an opportunity to share their questions and concerns with each other.

b. Address issues of the press and nonmembers (as set out above) who may be present. It is important to reinforce that this is not a "secret" meeting, but rather a gathering of the congregation, as a means of providing care and support to its members.

c. Provide brief self-introductions of those facilitating the meeting, including the bishop, any judicatory staff, and parish leaders. It is best for all leaders to introduce themselves because all members may not know them.

d. Give members an overview of the meeting by explaining the following in a sentence or two:

- There is some information to be shared with the congregation so that all members have accurate information.

- The majority of the meeting will be spent providing an opportunity for members to share questions and concerns.

- Many questions will be answered, but there is some information that cannot be shared because it involves personal information or a pastoral confidence.

- Before closing, next steps will be explored.

- Propose a timeframe for the meeting. Ask members if they will agree to work for two hours (or longer). Be sure to honor the timeframe. One of the facilitators should serve as timekeeper. If toward the end of the meeting members are very engaged and seem to have serious concerns that have not yet been addressed, ask the group if they would like to extend the ending time by fifteen or thirty minutes. It's best not to allow the meeting to run over without first receiving permission of the members.

3. An educational segment

This involves presenting three key principles learned from other congregations in the wake of misconduct. This is the most content-laden part of the meeting, which will be the focus of chapter 7.

4. Reading of disclosure statement

The disclosure statement is read by the bishop, a facilitator, or a parish leader, depending on whether the judicatory or parish is responsible for the response to misconduct.[8] The reader should be prepared to read the statement through two times. At the end of the statement, tell members when and who was previously informed of the misconduct, such as wardens, vestry, and staff. Be clear about what information was shared with them. In the wake of misconduct and erosion

---

8. Generally, a judicatory is responsible for the discipline of ordained leaders, and parish leaders are responsible for the response to lay misconduct. The bishop and judicatory staff can assist parish leaders in this response.

of trust, it is important for members to know if some individuals have been provided with more information than others. Generally, leaders should receive the same information as members—just a bit sooner. This should be made clear to prevent members from assuming that the wardens and vestry are keeping information from them.[9]

Directly after the reading of the disclosure statement, members may be invited to ask limited questions—only to seek clarification of the statement. Leaders and/or facilitators provide responses related *only* to clarification of the statement. Be careful that questions asked here do not extend to general questions, reactions, and comments about misconduct; these will all be gathered before providing any responses.

5. Gathering questions, comments, and concerns

An effective way for members to digest the disclosure statement they just heard is for members to listen to each other's questions and concerns without interruption by facilitators. This requires that the facilitators listen and gather the questions, comments, and concerns of members *before* responding to any of them.

There are a number of good reasons for gathering all of the members' questions and concerns before responding. First, emotions may be running high. There is a possibility that answering each question in turn can convert the meeting into a contentious "press conference" style event, rather than a conversation within a faith community. If members are angry about the misconduct, they may direct their anger at the meeting facilitators. The process of gathering questions helps avoid such dynamics.

This process allows members to build questions off of each other's and provides time to move beyond the initial questions of who, what, where, and when, to deeper questions such as: "Why did this happen here?" "How will this impact my community of faith?" "How does this affect my trust in myself and my relationship with

---

9. In some situations wardens and vestry members may need to hold some details in confidence. For example, if wardens are negotiating a severance package with a rector, not all details can be shared in the midst of negotiating. However, members could be told that the wardens are actively engaged in negotiation. It is likely that the bishop would also be involved in such negotiations.

God?" The first questions asked may not be the truly important questions. If questions are responded to in the order asked, there may not be time to ask or respond to the truly important ones. Listening to each other allows members to begin to hear the differences among their reactions to misconduct. This helps to make it okay to be different from others, while also recognizing commonalties in responses. Finally, this approach provides time for all members to reflect before speaking, and creates opportunity for introverts, who may need time to process before speaking, to participate.

How to gather questions and concerns

Tell members that all of their questions and concerns will be gathered and recorded on paper by facilitators before responses are offered.[10] Facilitators need to allow for *silence*. Some groups are slow to start voicing questions and concerns; others start right away and then have pauses between members' inquires. Allow about fifteen minutes to gather questions. To ensure that everyone can hear, a facilitator should repeat each question or comment, or pass a microphone to the member speaking.

When there seems to be a lull after having spent adequate time to gather questions and concerns, check to see if there is anything else on members' minds or in their hearts. Often a member will ask, "Are you going to give us some answers? If so, when?" If this happens, offer assurances that answers will be provided, but you just want to be sure there aren't any additional questions or concerns not yet expressed. After this type of exchange, the questions and concerns expressed can be those that are more meaningful and difficult for members to confront.

In this process of gathering, it may feel as though there are too many questions or concerns to address during this meeting, but you will discover that they generally fall into categories. Groupings of questions can often be answered by a few sentences of clear explanation. The common categories that members' questions fall into

---

10. It is preferable to record questions and concerns on paper rather than newsprint or a whiteboard. Posting questions and concerns publicly may inhibit some members from expressing themselves. Moreover, this can make it difficult for the facilitators to group the questions into categories if the walls are covered in newsprint.

are: clarification of the disclosure statement, disciplinary process set out by denomination's canons, involvement of secular authorities such as child protective services or police, identification of victim or complainant,[11] concerns about media, the practices and policies that were in effect that created the opportunity for misconduct to occur, what needs to change to prevent this from happening again, and what pastoral care, support, and services are being made available to the victim, complainant, offender, and their families. A form to assist facilitators in the gathering and categorizing of questions is provided in Appendix F.

Once the gathering of questions is complete, the bishop, facilitators, or leadership respond. Begin by affirming the differences in members' reactions to misconduct and how the ability to share these differences strengthens the community of faith, assuming that members did express differences. Ideally, more than one person responds to the list of questions so that the person(s) not currently responding has an opportunity to review the list of gathered questions and mentally compose the next response.

If the nature of the misconduct will likely lead to questions that are best answered by an expert in that subject matter (such as an accountant for embezzlement or an expert in child sexual abuse), it is best to have such an expert present throughout the disclosure meeting. As leaders respond to the gathered questions and concerns, the expert can be asked to respond to those questions that apply to his or her area of expertise.

Take care not to disclose any identifying information regarding the victim or complainant beyond that which was already disclosed in the disclosure statement. Be particularly careful if the gender has not been disclosed, as it is very easy to slip and reveal this information by using a pronoun, such as he or she and him or her.

If there is a statement for the press, read that to members in the context of responding to their questions and concerns. Knowing

---

11. This assumes that victims do not want their identity disclosed and may require a reminder that the focus should remain on the offender, not the identity of who was directly impacted, or who reported the matter to church leadership. When a victim does not want their identity disclosed, it may be necessary to ask members to refrain from speculation and use of a name to refer to the primary victim if members start to refer to the victim by name. Remind members that the facilitators will not confirm or deny the identity of a primary victim.

what they can expect to see or hear in the news can be reassuring—and prevents surprise.

After responding to the list of gathered questions and concerns, if time allows, the facilitators may wish to ask members if they have any additional concerns or questions. Chances are that by this point, most concerns have been raised and addressed.

6. Next steps

Next steps should be outlined before the meeting concludes. It is impossible to know all that will be needed to support the congregation in moving forward, but the congregation should be told what support is currently available to them and that as needs arise, appropriate responses will be provided. Encourage members to go to their wardens and vestry with needs and ideas of what will be helpful in moving forward. The role of these lay leaders is to listen and support members, and then determine if there are common needs being raised. It is essential that any personal stories shared by members with wardens and vestry be held in confidence unless a member expressly gives permission for their story to be shared with others.

Most importantly, the congregation should be assured that they will receive timely updated information as it becomes available, and that this meeting is not the only opportunity for community discussion about the misconduct.

Introduce some possible next steps that could move the congregation toward healing. This might include opportunities for sharing concerns in smaller ministry groups. Judicatory staff, a psychologist, and/or congregational leaders could facilitate these conversations. Certain members and groups within the congregation will be affected by misconduct in different ways—some will want additional opportunities to process and discuss the misconduct. Others will not. Appendix G contains a sample invitation to an additional opportunity to discuss misconduct.

Often members need time to reflect and discern what would be helpful in restoring trust. Leaders should be in ongoing communication with judicatory staff to decide next steps and tailor them to best meet the needs of this community.

Invite members to avail themselves of pastoral care and support. Describe the pastoral resources available and how members can access these resources. Access might be through a congregation's ordained leadership, a pastoral care team, lay leaders, and/or judicatory staff. Reiterate the importance for all members to take care of themselves. If they find themselves tense, sad, or irritable in the days to come, it may be that they are experiencing a reaction to having learned about misconduct in their church. For some members, facing misconduct in their church can open up wounds from past injuries and losses.

Facilitators might suggest a next step of providing support to children and youth of the parish, who are also affected by congregational misconduct. The disclosure statement might be revised for children and youth, and it may be appropriate to hold special meetings for children and youth. They, too, need accurate information and the opportunity to share questions and concerns. It is wise to have these meetings designed and facilitated by individuals who are knowledgeable in child and human development, such as a child psychologist. This may require a number of meetings since children and youth should be divided into age-appropriate groups for discussions.

Many congregations find it helpful to learn more about the power dynamics of misconduct and how to prevent further incidents. A relatively easy next step is to schedule a face-to-face training session for as many members as possible that addresses: power dynamics in ministerial relationships; the impact of congregational misconduct; the prevention, recognition, and response to suspected abuse of children, elders, or dependent adults; and policies and practices to promote healthy boundaries in a faith community. A live training session will not only provide content for a deeper understanding of the misconduct, but an additional opportunity for the community members to process the misconduct with each other.[12]

---

12. Training materials on some of these topics are available through Church Pension Group at *www.cpg.org*. Curricula for face-to-face training events as well as online training are available. Look for *Safeguarding God's Children* and *Safeguarding God's People—Exploitation*.

7. Closing with prayer

Be sure that if prayer is offered for the offender (or alleged offender), that prayer is also offered for the victim (or alleged victim). Sometimes due to oversight, only victims or offenders are included in prayer. This can cause division within the congregation and undermine the integrity of the disclosure process. This is a process not about taking sides, but disclosing accurate information. It is also appropriate to pray for the healing of all those who offend and all those who have been harmed by misconduct in faith communities. Remember not to use the victim's name.

ॐ

Disclosing misconduct to members of a congregation is essential to rebuild trust. Both the content of disclosure and the process of disclosure can impact the long-term vitality of a congregation.[13] Creating a safe space for members to process and share their reactions and concerns can be life giving. Careful planning and execution can make room for the Holy Spirit to transform and heal individual members and the congregation as a whole. Appendix H contains an outline of this entire disclosure process. Facilitators, bishops, judicatory staff and lay leaders can use it in planning and conducting a disclosure meeting in a congregation or other impacted communities.

---

13. This disclosure process can also be used to disclose misconduct to peer clergy who are impacted by a colleague's misconduct. Disclosure to clergy colleagues usually occurs after disclosure in the congregation. Clergy colleagues may experience betrayal when a peer engages in misconduct, often resulting in rumors, fear, anger, and sadness. Their reactions can be exacerbated if the judicatory fails to share accurate and timely information with these clergy. If clergy witness their peers undergoing canonical discipline without being told the basis for such discipline, their trust in the judicatory and its processes can erode.

7

Restoring Trust

EDUCATION AND INFORMATION

This chapter describes and explains in necessary detail the third important component of the disclosure meeting that was briefly identified as the "educational segment" of the meeting in the last chapter. This educational component includes three key principles for promoting healing after misconduct. Facilitators' understanding of these principles, including their theological basis, will enhance the facilitators' ability to communicate and effectively coordinate the disclosure and response process. These principles have been gleaned from numerous experiences addressing congregational misconduct.

In the absence of misconduct, these principles provide helpful insight for congregational leadership, lay and ordained. They can promote respectful and honest conversation on challenging issues in any congregation. In the wake of misconduct, these principles help members understand what they've been hearing, how they've been feeling, and why it is important to talk about misconduct in a faith community.

The three key principles are centered on: categories of information, responses to misconduct, and truth telling. All kinds of information flow through congregations after misconduct—facts, allegations, speculation, rumors, and opinions. Being aware of these *categories of information* helps members evaluate for themselves the quality of information they are receiving and reduces sharing of speculation and rumor. Discussing the ways *members respond* to misconduct helps them understand the dynamics at work in their congregation. It also gives them permission to share their feelings and validates that though each may feel very differently about the misconduct, they can still support and hold one another in community. *Truth telling* about misconduct is required to restore trust in relationships within the congregation. We are called to be in truthful, authentic, and right relationship with one another and God.

In the context of a disclosure meeting, a facilitator presents an overview of these principles. Additional information about these principles can be offered in response to members' questions and concerns. Generally, these principles are presented before the disclosure statement is read. In certain limited circumstances, these principles are best presented *after* the disclosure statement is read.[1]

CATEGORIES OF INFORMATION

In the wake of misconduct, or whenever there is stress and anxiety in a parish system, all sorts of information begins to circulate. It is helpful for members to be aware of which category of information a particular statement falls into. At any meeting the most effective way to present the five categories of information is to have newsprint or slides listing the categories and placed in a central location throughout the meeting. This encourages everyone to refer back to the list to indicate which category the information he or she is sharing falls into. Often members will refer to the categories of information when expressing their own concerns and feelings.

---

1. Generally, members have some idea that misconduct has occurred even before the disclosure statement is read. They may have learned about it from the press, seen things that raised suspicions, or may be openly talking about the misconduct while the formal response is just getting underway. In these situations, it is appropriate to follow the order outlined in chapter 6, in which these principles are shared before the disclosure statement is read. If, however, members have no idea that misconduct has occurred and reading the disclosure statement will be "breaking news," it makes sense to read the disclosure statement before sharing these three principles. In these situations, reverse the order of #3 and #4 in the Disclosure Meeting Outline as discussed in chapter 6 and found in Appendix H.

List the categories from top to bottom: facts, allegations, specu-lation, rumor, and finally opinions, viewpoints, and feelings. Give a brief explanation of each category based on the following:[2]

- **Facts:** An act or thing that actually happened or exists; some-thing that we know is true, not something that might or might not have happened
- **Allegations:** An assertion of a fact, a statement that has not yet been proven or disproven
- **Speculation:** A form of a guess or a hunch based on some infor-mation, with the risk that it is not true. Speculation is a natural function of our minds. When we have only partial information or there are gaps in information, our minds will naturally fill in the gaps because we are wired to make sense of our world. Our minds will create a story out of bits and pieces of information. In some cases, we may not be aware that we have filled in the gaps.
- **Rumor:** A popular story being repeated from person to person with no known authority for its truth or origin. Rumor can be based on speculation, and can sometimes be malicious.
- **Opinions, feelings, viewpoints:** Sometimes people express their opinions, feelings and viewpoints so often, assuredly, and loudly, that they start to sound like facts, when they are just one person's opinion, feeling, or viewpoint. Each member's opinions, feelings, and viewpoints are valid and to be honored, but this does not make them facts.

During a disclosure meeting, facilitators should try to clarify which category of information they are sharing when they speak about the misconduct. They should avoid sharing information that is speculation or rumor. (Most likely there is plenty of that infor-mation already circulating.) It can be helpful to explain that facil-itators, like members, may be tempted to speculate because there are some things that we just don't know and we are trying to figure them out.

---

2. Definitions for the first four categories are loosely based on definitions found in *Ballentine's Law Dictionary, 3rd edition*, edited by James Ballentine and William Anderson (Rochester, NY: The Lawyers Co-Operative Publishing Company, 1969).

RESPONSES TO MISCONDUCT

The next key principle to present is the variety of ways members and congregations react to misconduct. This does three things: it affirms for individual members that no matter how they are feeling, such feelings are valid, making them more likely to share their experiences with each other; it provides a framework for understanding why members may be reacting very differently from one another; and gives permission for members to support and hold each other in community even though they may have drastically different responses to misconduct.

Members react to misconduct, or allegations of misconduct, in a number of ways including disbelief, shame, anger at the offender, anger at the bishop for imposing discipline, anger at others, blame of victim or person who reported the misconduct, and sadness. Individual members may find themselves reacting and feeling differently at different times.

Members may feel conflicted. Often this comes from knowing that the offender has served well, done wonderful ministry, and now has also engaged in misconduct. It is often very hard to hold both of these realities simultaneously. In addition to this internal conflict, it is natural for there to be divisions within a congregation following misconduct.

For some, the misconduct may bring to the forefront prior experiences of betrayal, loss, or victimization in their lives. These prior experiences may or may not have occurred in a church setting.

Many congregations that have experienced misconduct have moved forward, restored trust, and are now healthy, vital communities of faith actively engaged in God's mission. The facilitator should provide assurance that all shall be well, regardless of what members are feeling and however the congregation is reacting. Individuals and the congregation will move through these challenges and heal, if the work of restoring trust is engaged.[3]

TRUTH TELLING

The final principle to present is why it is essential for congregations to talk about misconduct. This involves sharing some theology as

---

3. Chapter 1 includes an in-depth description of how members as individuals, and congregations as communities, respond to misconduct.

well as the consequences that follow when misconduct is not disclosed in a congregation.

As Christians we are called into authentic relationship with God and each other. Authentic relationships have integrity and are built on honest and accurate information. It is imperative that all members of a congregation have accurate information about the congregation. This includes all aspects of congregational life—ministry and mission, budget, pledging, outreach, church school attendance, as well as misconduct.

The implications of not openly discussing misconduct in a congregation are far reaching and long lasting. Failure to disclose misconduct sets up power differentials between those members who know about the misconduct and those who do not, creating an "in" group and an "out" group. In such cases, there will be secrets; members learn that the congregation does not talk about difficult topics; members may self-censor what they share with others in the congregation. When we can't talk about the brokenness that underlies misconduct, members become reluctant to share their own brokenness with others.

To restore trust, it is necessary to face and openly discuss misconduct. It is impossible to build trust in a faith community where individuals cannot express certain feelings and opinions, or explore their own brokenness and sinfulness. Open discussion of misconduct signals a community's resilience, health, and capacity to engage challenging topics. It encourages honest communication among members. This is an important principle for all members to understand. Some will mistakenly believe that misconduct is a private matter, just between the offender and primary victim; that the congregation should move forward and stop putting energy into talking about what's over and done with. A congregation needs to appreciate that rebuilding trust requires disclosing and talking about misconduct.

All congregations can benefit from understanding the principles regarding categories of information, responses to misconduct, and the necessity of truth telling. However, these principles are especially helpful to individuals and congregations in the wake of misconduct. In the context of a disclosure meeting, they promote an understanding of why talking about and working through the impact of misconduct is essential for well-being and wholeness, individually as members, and corporately as a community of faith.

8

The Wilderness

WANDERING WITH INTENTION

Rarely will allegations of misconduct be resolved so quickly that a congregation learns of the allegations and the final resolution of those allegations all at once. Typically, there is a disclosure meeting to inform members that allegations are pending and it isn't until weeks or months later that the matter is brought to final resolution. This time while the matter is pending can be a bewildering period for members and the congregation as a whole. Members are waiting. They may be waiting for the results of an investigation, for the canonical disciplinary process to conclude, to learn the consequence the offender faces, or whether the bishop will allow the priest to continue to serve or return to the parish.[1] This is a time of unknowing. Members may be tempted to speculate, to "fill in the blanks" where there is missing (or yet to be known) information.

This in-between time can be particularly unsettling because not only do members need to grapple with potential betrayal and all the varying reactions, they need to wait to get the full story. Waiting is hard. We live in a culture of impatience; we don't get much practice in waiting patiently. Members may find their peace of mind assaulted by thoughts of "What if . . . ?" and spend energy playing out numerous options. What was once familiar and a source of comfort in the parish may now seem unfamiliar. Longtime friends react

---

1. This time can also feel like the wilderness to primary victims and alleged offenders, who are also living with the questions of what will happen.

to the news of misconduct in surprising ways; sometimes they can't be present to provide support as they normally would. Members may actively work to prove or disprove the allegations by attempting to ascertain facts or provide financial assistance to the alleged offender or the church. Members should be assured that resources are being devoted to determine the facts and it is best if members leave this to others who are outside of the congregation.

Some of the challenges and gifts of this in-between time are akin to those of being in the wilderness. Consider Jesus's forty days in the wilderness or the Israelites' forty years of wandering. In both of these wilderness experiences, there was an element of aloneness (in the feeling of being alone or actually being alone), an unknown outcome or resolution, and an unknown timeframe. The Israelites were fearful, complained bitterly, disrespected their leader, and wanted to go back to Egypt—to return to what they knew. It's common for members to wish to return to the way things were before the issue of misconduct was brought to light. This is not possible—the impact of misconduct changes and transforms members and congregations as well. It can be very tempting to respond to the wilderness as the Israelites did.

Jesus had his own time in the wilderness. During that time Jesus had steadfast faith in God from whom he derived strength and wisdom. Jesus also relied on the power of God's Word. Each time he was tempted, he replied with, "It is written . . ."[2] and quoted Scripture. We too can intentionally engage the practices modeled by Jesus in the wilderness: steadfast faith and reliance on Scripture.

There are a multitude of wonderful passages that address waiting, wilderness, and faith, such as Psalm 62:5–8:

For God alone my soul waits in
   silence,
    for my hope is from him.
He alone is my rock and my
   salvation,
    my fortress; I shall not be
   shaken.

---

2. Matthew 4:4, 7, 10.

On God rests my deliverance and
> my honor;
> my mighty rock, my refuge is
> in God.
Trust in him at all times,
> O people;
> pour out your heart
> before him;
> God is a refuge for us.

This time in the wilderness can be a time of rich spiritual growth and formation. There are numerous approaches that individual members or groups within a congregation might engage, including:

- bible study with a focus on waiting; writing one's own prayer for this time, or writing prayers in small ministry groups and sharing them with others;
- inserting an additional prayer in the Prayers of the People at each liturgy, much as parishes in search of new rector might add a prayer for their time of transition;
- establishing prayer partners and/or conversation partners in which members engage in ongoing conversation with another about what they are learning about themselves during this time in the wilderness; and
- beginning the monastic practice of praying the psalms that speak to waiting, faith, and journeying in the wilderness.

In all cases, the focus remains on the members' learnings about themselves, not the misconduct and dynamics in the congregation,

Other strategies for moving through this time might include inviting members of another congregation who have already lived through such a time to share their experiences, hopes, and assurances that it is possible to move through this in-between time and deepen one's relationship with God and each other. Leaders might offer regular reminders to the congregation to hold each other in Christian community while traveling through the wilderness, regardless of how individual members are responding to the news of misconduct.

If individual members or the congregation as a whole just can't seem to help themselves from thinking about, worrying about, or perseverating on the misconduct, it can be helpful to set aside a specific period of time (for example, fifteen minutes) to focus on the misconduct for only that period of time and then very intentionally engage focus on another topic.

All members should be urged to pay attention to caring for themselves during this time. Repeated reminders to be gentle on one's self and other members can be helpful. Self-care encompasses not only physical, cognitive, and emotional well-being, but also spiritual well-being. As members care for themselves during this time, some may find they need to establish new boundaries—perhaps they need to step back and decrease their degree of involvement with church ministries. For instance, a member may feel that he or she just cannot sing right now and may need to take a break from participation in the choir.

Some members may need to take a "time out" from all involvement in the life of the church, including worship. As members care for their spiritual well-being, some may need to worship in a different setting to be able to focus on their relationship with God. These are very difficult and painful decisions; family members may find themselves worshiping at different parishes. It does not necessarily mean that these members are leaving the parish—it's just that for now, they need some space. This can be hard for other members to understand; they may feel abandoned, angry, sad, or a combination of feelings when a member absents him or herself from the congregation. This is a time when it is essential that all members honor the varying responses of members and continue to hold each other in community—even those who are physically absent.

A key question all members ask is, "How long will it take to know the outcome? How long will we be in this wilderness?" And the answer is, not as long as the Israelites, but most likely longer than the forty days Jesus spent in the wilderness. Even when judicatory disciplinary processes move as quickly as possible, it is likely to take some time. These are important matters, and while time is of the essence, these processes should not be conducted in a hurried manner. Before a matter is brought to conclusion, there will likely be additional information that can be shared with the congregation that can reduce, to some extent, the sense of being alone in the wilderness.

Even when a disciplinary action is brought to conclusion, the facts as to exactly what happened may remain unclear. Congregations need to restore trust and move toward closure even with this lack of clarity. The greatest degree of clarity regarding facts occurs when the offender admits to facts that constitute misconduct, and those facts correspond to the complainant's allegations. Although the facts may be difficult for members to hear, there can at least be a common understanding as to what transpired.

Lack of clarity and unresolved allegations can result when a judicatory terminates an investigation because the alleged offender surrenders his or her leadership role, or in secular court when a case is closed or dismissed without a clear finding of the facts. Even in cases where a court (ecclesiastical or secular) makes findings of facts, if the offender or complainant asserts that those facts are not accurate, there remains a degree of uncertainty as to what happened. Members need to find closure without having the benefit of conclusively knowing all the facts. This requires faith—to live with the unknown.

Members and congregations have a choice: they can spend this in-between time of waiting for resolution aimlessly wandering in the wilderness or journeying through the wilderness with intention. Even if the matter is resolved with clarity, and the facts are indisputedly clear, members will have varying reactions to the misconduct, requiring work to restore trust in the congregation. For many congregations, venturing into uncharted waters has not been done with intention in the past. As congregations enter this new territory, they and their members can be transformed. The experience of Christian fellowship can be enhanced.

Like the Israelites, we might want to go back to what our church and we were like before misconduct, but we can't. In essence, there is a death of the old way of being while something new is being born. With intentional work and focus on restoring trust, what is born can be a community of deeper faith, greater authenticity in relationships, in which members share an enhanced desire to engage as active members of the congregation.

The Tip of the Iceberg

Spiritual and
Emotional Abuse

Spiritual and emotional abuse is a distinctive form of congregational misconduct, requiring a distinctive response. It is often much harder to recognize than sexual, physical, or financial abuse. In some cases, members of a congregation slowly reveal spiritual and emotional abuse only after the offender has departed and a new, trusted ordained leader is serving the congregation. By then, targeted victims of the abuse may have left the congregation, and trust among the remaining members is diminished.

Spiritual and emotional abuse can be perpetrated by laity, but is more often perpetrated by clergy due to their greater "spiritual" authority. It can happen in private settings where no one else witnesses the abuse, or public settings where the entire congregation witnesses the abuse. Those who are the first to report these abusive behaviors may find their concerns dismissed by wardens, vestry, and even judicatory leaders. In cases of spiritual and emotional abuse, there are likely more primary victims than other forms of congregational misconduct.

Due to the unique nature of spiritual and emotional abuse, the process to disclose and respond to this form of abuse is modified. This modified process is tailored to meet the needs of members of congregations who have endured such abuse.

EXAMPLES OF SPIRITUAL AND EMOTIONAL ABUSE

While there can be a single instance of spiritual and emotional abuse, most often this form of abuse consists of a pattern of behavior. It can originate from the rector's need to control activities, information, and relationships within the congregation. An abuse of authority can take many forms: making theological statements of exclusion not based on denominational doctrine, ostracizing members, and forcing members out of leadership positions to replace them with members who will "rubber stamp" whatever the rector wants.

Spiritually and emotionally abusive conduct can encompass a wide variety of behavioral patterns, and the following are but some examples of such abusive interactions:

- a rector who yells at a church school teacher during coffee hour for having given gifts to children in her class;
- a rector who controls the content of vestry meeting agendas and determines who is permitted to speak at such meetings;
- a rector who repeatedly reminds staff members that he or she has the authority to fire them;
- a rector who directs staff to engage in questionable behaviors by starting rumors about "troublesome" parishioners;
- a rector who instructs a member from the pulpit during a sermon to leave worship because the member's skirt is too short;
- a rector who privately tells a lay leader who disagrees with him that a rector has the power to excommunicate him from the church[1];
- a rector who leaves calling cards, prayers, and trinkets at a gravesite after family members ask that this stop;
- a rector who emails all members to tell them to refrain from calling on church members whose first child had just died of SIDS[2] because the couple wanted time alone to grieve—later members learn that the couple did not make that request and that it was

---

1. This statement is false. It reflects the rector's abuse of power in an untoward effort to seek compliance from a lay leader.

2. Sudden Infant Death Syndrome.

the love, prayers, and companionship (of those who violated the rector's edict) that supported the couple in their grief.

Other examples include:

- telling a parishioner that the funeral of her husband was invalid because it was performed by an ordained woman rather than a man;

- announcing and identifying members who will no longer be a part of the congregation until they terminate familial relationships with relatives who are gay; and

- telling members that the bishop (judicatory) is "out to get me" (the ordained leader) and this congregation, so if anyone goes to the bishop, the bishop will "take over" the parish and perhaps close the church.

If one considers a single example from the interactions listed above, in isolation, it may not appear to be an abuse of power and authority. However, when the list of interactions is viewed as a whole, a pattern of abusive behavior becomes clear. Typically, the initial reports of spiritual and emotional abuse consist only of one or two troubling interactions with a cleric. Imagine a judicatory receiving reports that a rector yelled at a church school teacher during coffee hour, and controls the content and speakers at vestry meetings. Taken individually, these acts do not present a clear-cut case of abuse of authority. Yet when the entire pattern is seen as a whole, they certainly do.

Initial reports of spiritual and emotional abuse may be dismissed by bishops and Title IV Intake Officers. Intake Officers have the authority to dismiss an intake if it does not appear to constitute an offense, provided the bishop consents.[3]

Initially, distinguishing spiritual and emotional abuse from other dynamics in a congregation can be challenging; congregational systems make recognizing this form of abuse very difficult. A newly

---

3. See Canon IV.6.4.

called rector may find patterns of behavior in a parish that need to change to bring new order and healthy boundaries to the parish system. These patterns may have developed during the interim period when the congregation was searching for its new rector, or may have been in effect for decades. When the new rector attempts to change these established patterns, there is likely to be push back from staff and members who resist this change, even when that change is healthy for the congregation as a whole. The push back may stem from the discomfort that accompanies change, or from fear of losing power and authority as a result of change. Members who raise initial concerns regarding spiritual and emotional abuse may be pushing back against the rector's appropriate use of authority as he or she begins to make changes to enhance the health of the parish system. Creating this kind of change is hard work for any leader; it requires a high degree of skill and emotional intelligence to navigate the intricacies of a parish system and implement change.

Consider a congregation where for many years the church administrator has been the go-to person for all pastoral needs of its members. When someone dies, the family contacts the church administrator, who does all the work to set up the funeral service, including meeting with the family and communicating with the funeral home. The rector may learn of a member's death only when the church administrator tells the rector the time and details of the funeral service, which have already been arranged and bulletins printed.

When a new rector appropriately tries to change this pattern, a number of things can, and likely will, happen. Imagine what happens when the new rector tells the church administrator, "From now on, I will handle all pastoral concerns of members. When a member calls, that call is to be forwarded to me. When a member dies, I will meet with the family and work with the funeral home to make the arrangements. I'll let you know of the details so you can prepare the service bulletin." The church administrator may perceive this as being yelled at, regardless of the rector's tone of voice, and may interpret this as reflecting a lack of concern for members' pastoral needs.

The church administrator may share his or her concerns with members of the congregation, the wardens, and vestry. This can quickly lead to division, as some will support their new rector, while others may start to see all of the rector's decisions as an attempt to take power away from those who have served faithfully and as disregard for members' pastoral concerns. Leaders may try to support their new rector and begin to view the church administrator, and others who object to the new rector, as troublesome and resistant to change. Members who are harmed by the rector's behavior may feel further distressed when their lay leaders do not take their concerns seriously.

The rector may be attempting to appropriately exercise authority, or these may be the first reported instances of spiritual and emotional abuse. Without further information about the rector's behavior and the church's previous operating system, it can be impossible to ascertain whether this is abusive behavior or the appropriate exercise of the rector's authority. Often, it will take time and multiple members voicing concerns before the judiciary can determine if the rector's behavior is abusive, thereby justifying intervention. In these situations, the newly called rector may never develop relationships or earn the trust of some members of the congregation.

Conversely, when a rector has had a lengthy tenure in a congregation, it may take longer for members to report spiritual and emotional abuse to judicatory leaders. Rectors who serve congregations for a lengthy tenure build relationships with members and provide pastoral care at key moments in members' lives. It is this relationship and trust that makes it hard for members to recognize that the trusted leader is, or was, abusing power and authority over them. Moreover, if the abusive behaviors develop gradually, members may become accustomed to the inappropriate behavior and diminish its seriousness: "Oh, that's just our rector's way of being funny," or "Wait until next month, s/he will be yelling at someone else and you will be the favorite." In many cases, it isn't until a new priest begins to serve a congregation that members begin to recognize the abusive nature of their former rector's behavior.

THE IMPACT ON LAY LEADERSHIP

Spiritual and emotional abuse by a priest impacts a congregation's lay leadership in specific ways. Perhaps most importantly, the overall capacity of lay leadership is diminished when the priest is controlling; rather than leading as part of a team with laity, the priest stifles and restricts the ability of laity to lead. Even congregations that once had strong lay leadership may find that the strong leaders, who would not go along with the priest's dictates, were pushed out of leadership positions or became the targets of the priest's abuse. Often, able leaders who find themselves in positions where they cannot be effective will voluntarily step down from those leadership positions and find ways to effect change elsewhere.

Effective wardens and vestries may be sabotaged as the rector works to have greater control throughout the congregational system. These lay leaders may inaccurately be told that things for which they were responsible now fall within the authority of the rector; the rector may dismantle effective committee structures. A rector might demand that all matters be discussed directly with the rector rather than in lay leadership teams. Healthy communication patterns may be shut down.

Leaders may give a new rector who is controlling and demanding the benefit of the doubt and support the rector in those demands. Lay leaders have a strong desire for their new rector to be successful. The parish may have just been through a long search process. Members harmed by the rector's behavior may begin to blame lay leaders for not intervening sooner. These lay leaders, who can become the target of other members' anger, may be ostracized. These leaders need support as the work to rebuild trust proceeds.

In congregations where spiritual and emotional abuse occurred during a long rectorship, it is unlikely that there are experienced and knowledgeable lay leaders. Not only have the current members serving in leadership positions been prevented from being effective, there may be no members in the parish who know how wardens, vestry, and officers are supposed to function. Leadership training and education in such instances are essential. It is likely that members have incorrect understandings and assumptions about the roles and authority of lay leaders.

MULTIPLE PRIMARY VICTIMS

In the presence of spiritual and emotional abuse, it is likely there are many more primary victims directly impacted by a priest's abuse of authority than with other forms of congregational misconduct. While possible, it is unlikely for there to be only one or two members directly impacted. Often, whatever is reported to the judiciary is just the tip of the iceberg—the majority of episodes of abuse are not disclosed until members share those incidents with each other in a facilitated disclosure process.

When members begin to realize that they and perhaps others in the congregation have been victimized, they will likely experience a number of reactions. Some of these reactions are similar to those experienced with other forms of congregational misconduct, while others are somewhat different. Some members will suffer great shame from having allowed themselves, as adults, to be victimized in this way. This can be particularly true for those serving in lay leadership positions. For some, this shame will be combined with guilt when they begin to see that they colluded with an abusive leader— perhaps dismissing concerns raised early on by other members in the congregation. Some may come to realize that they benefited from the rector's abuse by having been placed in a position of leadership or stature by the rector.

Members who were unaware that others were harmed by the rector's behavior may feel isolated and guilty. Often these members have had positive experiences with the rector. These members may feel quite alone if the majority of members have been targets of the rector's abusive behaviors. Those whose involvement in the life of the congregation has been limited to attendance of worship may be completely unaware of the destructive behaviors and harm.

DISCLOSURE OF SPIRITUAL AND EMOTIONAL ABUSE

The process of disclosing spiritual and emotional abuse differs from the process to disclose other forms of abuse. Here, at least two distinct types of disclosure meetings are needed. The first, a *primary disclosure meeting*, is where members first learn from the judicatory that allegations of spiritual and emotional abuse have been raised. This meeting is similar to disclosure meetings for other forms of misconduct (described in chapter 6), with one exception—the disclosure statement is very general. It is impossible to craft a single disclosure statement regarding spiritual and emotional abuse because many members likely have their own unique stories of abuse. At a *secondary disclosure meeting*, members learn from each other the substance of the allegations and their stories of abuse.

At the primary disclosure meeting, the judicatory discloses the fact that misconduct has been alleged and that there is (or is not) a canonical disciplinary action pending. In terms of disclosing the content of the misconduct, the judicatory can only draft a very general statement, which is an overview of the situation, such as: "The bishop has been made aware that your rector engaged in a pattern of behavior that has been hurtful to some members of the congregation."

Unlike other forms of misconduct, the judicatory cannot share the details of incidents, as that would likely identify primary victims or the person(s) who reported the misconduct. In addition, it is much more difficult for a judicatory to disclose a pattern of behaviors when only a small fraction of those behaviors have likely been reported to the judicatory. Moreover, if individual instances are disclosed that reveal a pattern of abuse only when combined with other instances, members who are unaware of the nature of spiritual and emotional abuse may begin to justify and rationalize each instance of the rector's behavior. They are not able to recognize the overall pattern of abuse. When members, rather than the judicatory, share their experiences and the impact these experiences had on them, other members more readily recognize the pattern of abuse.

After the primary disclosure meeting, a secondary disclosure meeting is essential.[4] At this meeting members disclose their own experiences of abuse to one another. This provides all members with

---

4. It is inadvisable to try to combine these two meetings into one. A combined meeting runs the risk of requiring members to process too much at one time. This can have the effect of diminishing each person's ability to access information on an affective level because they are focused on processing information on a cognitive level. Reflecting on one's own experiences of abuse, and feelings about those experiences, is a significantly different task than discussing and asking questions about the denomination's disciplinary process.

the same information and opens up opportunities for members to begin to minister to each other, recognize ways they may have contributed to other members' pain, and begin to make amends for any harm their behaviors caused, even if they did not intend that harm.

Many aspects of planning the secondary disclosure meeting are the same as planning a primary disclosure meeting. The content of chapter 6 (planning a disclosure meeting) is applicable to planning this secondary meeting with respect to the following: facilitators, working with wardens and vestry to schedule the meeting, inviting members to attend, and room setup. Due to the nature of spiritual and emotional abuse, facilitators should be aware that many members present at the meeting are likely to be primary victims of the misconduct.

OUTLINE FOR SECONDARY DISCLOSURE MEETING(S)

While similar to the disclosure meeting described in chapter 6, some components of a secondary disclosure meeting are unique. Like a primary disclosure meeting, a secondary meeting opens with prayer, followed by introductory matters and an educational segment on the three key principles (as discussed in chapter 7). The bulk of the meeting then consists of three components that are specific to secondary disclosure meetings for spiritual and emotional abuse: (a) guidelines for conversation and sharing, (b) sharing of members' experiences with each other, and (c) reflections by facilitators. The secondary meeting then closes as other disclosure meetings do, with next steps and prayer.

1. Opening prayer and introductory matters

These components are similar to those of a disclosure meeting for any form of misconduct (described in chapter 6), with minor modifications to the introductory matters; the judicatory's disclosure statement is read as an explanation for why members are gathered for this disclosure meeting, and facilitators explain that the majority of the time will be an opportunity for members to share their own stories and experiences with each other. Facilitators will provide guidelines to help frame that time of sharing.

2. Education: Three key principles

The three key principles are the same as those presented in any type of disclosure meeting. In secondary disclosure meetings, this content helps create a safe environment for members to share their stories. If there has already been a primary disclosure meeting at which members were introduced to the three key principles, an overview of the principles will suffice, but pay particular attention to the importance of differences. (See chapter 7 for more information.)

It is essential for members to know that their differing experiences and reactions to the rector's behavior will not tear apart their faith community. The congregation can hold each other in community even when there are disagreements. In cases of spiritual and emotional abuse, it is helpful to explain that unlike financial misconduct, where there is one set of facts that can be shared with all members, here there are many sets of facts as experienced by different members—spiritual and emotional abuse consists of a pattern of behavior with multiple events and primary victims.

To further assist members in understanding their differing experiences and reactions, it can be helpful to ask them to imagine a sudden event happening right before them now. Point out that even if they all witnessed one event at the same time, there would be as many different ways to explain that event as there are people in the room. It is natural for people to perceive and respond to events differently from one another.

Guidelines for Conversation and Sharing

Guidelines help create a safe environment for members to risk sharing their experiences with each other. They are presented after the three key principles. If a congregation has a behavioral covenant or set of guidelines it already uses to engage in challenging conversations, those guidelines (perhaps with minor modification) may work well. The following guidelines have been particularly helpful to congregations during secondary disclosure meetings:

- **Engage in a conversation, not a debate.** This is about each member hearing the others' experiences. All experiences and opinions are valid; this is not about trying to convince others that one position is better or more valid than another.

- **Listen and be present.** When members are not sharing their own experiences, they are ministering to each other by being present and actively listening to what others are sharing. This is a gift that can be hard to find in our everyday lives.

- **Speak for yourself.** Each member is invited to speak from his or her own personal experience. Remind members of the importance of using "I statements." Request that members refrain from speaking for groups, even if that member is part of a group, for example, refrain from stating, "The entire choir feels. . . ."

- **If you speak a word of criticism, you are invited to speak a word of support.** This guideline reflects the reality that each of us has the capacity to do good and each of us makes mistakes along the way; it is important to reaffirm this duality.

- **Listen for ways that your actions may have caused harm to another.** Invite members to be open to hear if their actions negatively impacted another, even if their intentions were good. Recognizing how we may have hurt others is an essential step toward restoring trust.

After a brief explanation of each guideline, ask that those present abide by these guidelines for this conversation. Seek an affirmation from all those present. Have a flip chart, newsprint, or slides with these five guidelines prepared before the meeting starts. Leave the list in a prominent location throughout the meeting as a visual reminder.

3. Sharing experiences

Sharing of members' experiences with each other is the bulk of the meeting. At this point, the focus shifts away from the facilitators to the members. Facilitators need to be comfortable with silence, as it may take some congregations a few moments to start sharing. During this part of the meeting, the facilitators' role is to support those who are sharing by modeling attentive listening while being aware of the other members. Facilitators should be slow to intervene if members fail to follow a guideline. Given the opportunity, many congregations have members who will point out when a guideline is not being followed—in essence, the community will self-correct. Allowing self-correction helps to enhance the capacity of the community to engage in challenging conversations.

While unusual, there are some congregations that lack the ability to follow the guidelines. The meeting starts to go off track; members begin to repeatedly blame or shame each other, raise their voices, and debate rather than listen. If this happens, facilitators can stop the conversation, invite members to join in prayer, and pray for the presence of the Holy Spirit in the conversation.

As a secondary disclosure meeting progresses, facilitators work to ensure that all present have an opportunity to share their experiences. Facilitators may need to gently remind vocal members to refrain from repeated sharing until everyone who wishes to share has done so. It is also the work of facilitators to make it clear that no one is obligated to share their story. Some members only need to hear what others have experienced. Every member's presence helps support the community—whether or not they share their story.

4. Facilitators' reflections

After the sharing of members' stories is brought to a close, facilitators reflect what they witnessed. Facilitators could name the emotions that were expressed, point out the significant differences of members' experiences, state themes that emerged (if any emerged), and provide encouragement for the members' good and hard work. If members cared for each other, made space for differences, and honored their differences, this should be pointed out. These are important capacities for a congregation as it moves forward in the wake of misconduct.

5. Next steps and closing prayer

Typically, both these components follow the same format used in other disclosure meetings as described in chapter 6. If there are clear next steps, such as further meetings scheduled or a next phase of disciplinary action, these should be identified at this point. As members have already worked hard during this meeting, this is not the time to decide details of next steps. Generally, it is wise to encourage members to go to their wardens and vestry members with concerns, invite members to use the pastoral care resources available to them, and explore whether children and youth or other groups within the congregation need support. Typically it is beneficial to provide a brief overview of boundaries, power, and roles in a congregation.

MODIFICATION FOR LARGER CONGREGATIONS

In small congregations, one secondary disclosure meeting will provide ample opportunity for all members to share their experiences. In larger congregations, however, it may be necessary to hold a series of secondary disclosure meetings to provide this opportunity for all members.

It is ideal to schedule a series of such meetings with twenty to thirty-five members invited per meeting. Members are invited based on the ministries in which they are engaged. The first meeting includes vestry, wardens, and their spouses/partners; another meeting includes the search committee and spouses/partners; and other meetings include members of active ministry groups within the congregation such as the choir. It is also important to have at least one secondary disclosure meeting that is open to all members. This provides an opportunity for all members to participate, including those whose only involvement in the life of the congregation is attending worship. Ideally a few representatives of the wardens and vestry attend each such meeting. This helps lay leaders support all members and get an overall picture of what is happening in their congregation.

In the wake of misconduct, it is important for members to hear other members' experiences and how they have been impacted. When there is a series of secondary disclosure meetings, members hear only those experiences that were shared in the meeting they attended. To address this, it is necessary to conclude the series of secondary disclosure meetings with a gathering of the entire congregation.

The structure for the gathering of the congregation is different from the other disclosure meetings. Here, most members will listen and support the few members who are asked ahead of time to share their experiences with the congregations. Facilitators and leaders decide together which members are invited to share with the entire congregation. It is critical that the members asked to share represent the full range of diversity of members' experiences as expressed throughout the series of secondary disclosure meetings. It is also important to have diversity in terms of gender, age, worship service regularly attended, ministry groups, wardens, and vestry.

These members are asked to share their experiences in three to four minutes. Providing this timeframe ensures that the meeting will not get bogged down, and encourages members to reflect and share what they believe are the essential pieces of their stories.

At the gathering of the congregation, facilitators explain how this meeting is different from the disclosure meetings that many of the members already attended. Members are asked to listen and be fully present to those who have been asked to share. One at a time, the pre-identified members share their stories. Often these members will need an extra minute or two. It is wise for facilitators to be flexible and allow a couple of extra minutes, and yet be aware of the need to keep the meeting moving.

Offering a congregation the opportunity to engage in a series of secondary disclosure meetings followed by a gathering of the entire congregation is ambitious and takes considerable time and energy, but is a process that can promote restoration of trust and wholeness in the wake of misconduct. The presence of the Holy Spirit is palpable at the gathering of a congregation when members share their experiences, how they were impacted, and take responsibility for any harm caused by their inability to appreciate and honor differing experiences of members; often it is these same members who were blaming and shaming others at a secondary disclosure meeting. Witnessing the transformative acts of grace as these members ask for forgiveness from the congregation is not only inspiring, it reassures the congregation that it has the capacity to continue the hard work of restoring trust.

A View from the Pew
The Role of Lay Leaders

All congregational leaders, regardless of their experience and ability, face challenges following misconduct. Lay leaders are on site; they are present in the parish on a day-to-day basis. Members will look to these leaders to find meaning in the unexpected events, and may disclose personal information to them. In addition, these leaders may become the targets of members' displaced anger and anxiety. Lay leaders are among those most impacted by misconduct in a congregation.

Consider a parish where the bishop puts a rector on administrative leave when allegations of sexual abuse are made. Without warning or notice, the wardens find themselves responsible for the care of the parish. This includes all day-to-day matters such as supervision of staff, locking and unlocking buildings, securing clergy for worship services, and ensuring that members' pastoral needs are met. In addition, lay leaders find themselves asking broader questions: What will happen to the parish? Will members leave? Will members continue to pay their pledge? Why is conflict emerging?

Lay leaders are called to engage these questions while simultaneously dealing with their own individual reactions to misconduct. In essence, lay leaders find themselves in dual roles—that of leader and that of impacted member. Leaders transition from having a view from the balcony and seeing the overall needs and dynamics of the congregation as a whole, to a view from the pew as a member in the midst of those needs and dynamics. This requires judicatory leaders to engage lay leaders in two ways: as colleagues in planning specific pastoral responses for the congregation,[1] and as individual members of a community that has been betrayed. The engagement of lay leaders has three prongs: equipping them to lead during this time, preparing them for the pastoral concerns that members will bring to them, and caring for the leadership team.

EQUIPPING LAY LEADERS

Judicatories can support lay leaders by providing education on the dynamics of congregations following misconduct. This helps the leaders know what to expect. It is equally important to provide them with the opportunity to process their own personal responses to misconduct *before* all members learn of the misconduct and begin to process their responses to misconduct.

Lay leaders and their congregations benefit when leaders understand the role of anxiety in a congregational system and the value of having non-anxious leaders. For some leaders, this may be the first time they focus on a congregation's emotional life and how the leaders' own emotions can impact a congregation. It is important not to overwhelm leaders with information, and yet having significant information on these dynamics will best support some.[2] It is natural for members of a group to look to their leaders to interpret situations and attribute meaning to events. This is particularly true in congregations under stress. An entire congregation benefits when lay leaders are calm, thoughtful, reflective, and grounded.

One way judicatories can equip lay leaders is to inform them of misconduct and provide them with opportunities to process their reactions *before* the misconduct is disclosed to the entire

---

1. Details as to the collaborative and consultative working relationship between judicatory leaders and lay leaders are articulated in the chapters outlining specific processes to respond to congregational misconduct.

2. Resources for lay leaders include: *Congregational Leadership in Anxious Times: Being Calm and Courageous No Matter What* by Peter L. Steinke (Herndon, VA: Alban Institute, 2006); *God's Tapestry: Understanding and Celebrating Differences* by William M. Kondrath (Herndon, VA: Alban Institute, 2008); and *Facing Feelings in Faith Communities* by William M. Kondrath (Herndon, VA: Alban Institute, 2013).

congregation. In essence, the judicatory invites the leadership team to a disclosure meeting before all other members are invited to such a meeting.[3] This gives leaders time to ponder the news of misconduct, begin to grapple with their own feelings, and learn how other members of the leadership team are responding before having to serve as a leader and provide pastoral support to other members of the congregation. It also gives leaders the experience of a disclosure meeting so they can better advise and assist in the planning of the congregational disclosure meeting.

To be effective, lay leaders need to know how to manage information regarding misconduct. Judicatories can provide assistance in working with the press and the importance of confidentiality.[4] Lay leaders are asked to hold in confidence all information regarding misconduct until that information is disclosed to all the members. From the time misconduct is disclosed to the lay leaders until it is disclosed to all members of the congregation, lay leaders have the burden of keeping this information to themselves. This is so all members learn the same information at the same time in the context of community—it is *not* to keep a secret from members. If lay leaders were to tell only some individual members about the misconduct, chances are that incomplete and possibly inaccurate information would begin to flow through the congregation in the form of rumor and speculation. To prevent this and provide support to members when they learn of the misconduct, lay leaders carry the burden of holding information in confidence.

Lay leaders also need to know how to respond to members' inquires and concerns. Members may be anxious, which can cause them to present their questions and concerns in more reactive ways than they normally would. Leaders need to know that they are not personally responsible for another member's anxiety, fear, and anger, and that they cannot "fix" the situation for others. What lay leaders *can* do is listen, be present, and hear the concerns and fears of the congregation. A leader can ask permission to share a member's

---

3. Informing lay leaders before other members of the congregation is incorporated into the process to disclose misconduct described in chapter 6.

4. Managing the flow of information and working with the media is discussed in chapters 5 and 6.

concerns with the rest of the leadership team. Leaders can assure members that they are not alone in their feelings of distress and that the leadership team is working closely with the judicatory as everyone walks with the parish through this challenging time. It is helpful for leaders to have a clear understanding of how triangulation can occur and learn strategies to avoid this destructive behavior.

It is critical for lay leaders to know when they are acting in their role of leader, and when they are acting and speaking as a member of the congregation. When members engage a lay leader in his or her capacity as a leader, it is appropriate for the leader to put the needs of the member before his or her own needs. Lay leaders need to listen and be present to the members. Concerned members may not feel heard if a lay leader is defensive and shows exasperation and frustration. This does not mean that lay leaders should not be authentic and express their true feelings, but it does mean that, as leaders, they should be encouraged to vent and process their own feelings among the leadership team or with resources outside of the congregation. In some cases, judicatory staff can provide these opportunities for lay leaders.

PREPARING FOR PASTORAL MATTERS

Members may begin to talk about past incidents of betrayal or victimization in their lives. For some leaders this can catch them by surprise and be unsettling. Some members will have substantially healed from these past incidents; for others the wounds will be raw. Some members will share these past events with others in the congregation—particularly the leaders.

In one congregation, a man who had years of experience in the corporate world was serving as a warden. He assured judicatory leaders and vestry members that no one would come to him with personal pastoral concerns because members did not see him as a pastoral resource, but rather as a good administrator. Within a week, a woman in the congregation shared with him that the misconduct reminded her of when she was sexually assaulted as a young woman. The warden was grateful that he had been prepared for this. He knew he couldn't fix anything for the member and just listened. When he asked if there was anything he could do to help, she replied

"No, I feel better just having been able to tell you all this. I'm sure our congregation will get through this."

CARING FOR LAY LEADERS

Judicatory leaders may need to repeatedly remind lay leaders that they need to take care of themselves. There will be greater demands on their time and attention—leaders may have to set boundaries as to when and how often they will be available to other members and the parish. Leading a congregation after misconduct is a process that takes time—leaders should care for themselves so they can be effective for the long haul.

In addition, lay leaders should know what resources are available to them in case they find themselves struggling with anxiety, fear, anger, or isolation stemming from the misconduct. If these reactions to misconduct begin to interfere with the quality of relationships with friends and family, or a leader's ability to attend to employment or lead, then it is time for extra support. In some instances it may be appropriate for a judicatory to provide a certain number of supportive therapeutic counseling sessions for a lay leader, if the leader does not otherwise have access to such resource.

Judicatory leaders can care for lay leaders by providing perspective when the going gets tough. Parish leadership teams benefit from knowing that there are likely to be moments when things seem to be falling apart. In fact, it may seem like a disaster. Judicatories can assure these leaders that although it may feel like a disaster, it is most likely an indication that there is more work to do before trust is restored.

Reminding lay leaders of what we know as Christians can also provide perspective. We are people of hope in the face of death; we are people of the resurrection. In some congregations the restorative work after misconduct yields recognition that an old way of being is dying. This is a loss to be mourned, and this death may be necessary for new life to emerge in the congregation. This can be an exciting and challenging time to be a leader in a congregation. Often, not only do leaders grow more fully into their leadership roles, they become a more supportive functioning team and can experience a deeper understanding of their call to serve as a leader.

11

᏶ᎥᎥᎵ

The Victims and Offenders

CARE AND SUPPORT

t is essential that the utmost care and support be offered to primary victims (those directly impacted by misconduct) and their families, as well as those who offend or are alleged to have offended. While all members of a congregation are affected by misconduct, for those directly impacted (the child who was sexually abused, the woman with whom the rector sexualized a relationship) special attention is needed to ensure they are treated with dignity and respect. Those who offend also require special care.

It is generally recognized that victims of misconduct in congregations need care. The need to care for and support clergy and others who offend is not as readily appreciated. Yet, the work we are called to do as Christians, to reconcile and restore all of God's creation to one another and God, includes caring for offenders.

The Episcopal Church's disciplinary canons include specific provisions that apply to primary victims, complainants, and clergy who offend or are alleged to have offended. The canons do not address offenses committed by laity.[1]

---

1. A full explanation and description of the Title IV disciplinary process is outside the focus of this book. Training materials on this topic can be found on the Episcopal Church in Connecticut's website at *www.ctepiscopal.org*.

The canons explicitly require bishops to provide an appropriate pastoral response to all individuals and communities affected by clergy misconduct, not just primary victims and ordained offenders.[2]

At times, the needs, desires, and interests of the primary victim and offender may differ from those of the congregation. While seeking to support the primary victim and offender, it is also the work of the judicatory to restore trust in a congregation after misconduct. This may require taking steps that both the primary victim and offender object to. It is essential that the judicatory design appropriate responses for all those impacted so as to mitigate harm those responses may cause a primary victim or offender. Neither the primary victim nor offender should dictate the response provided to members of a congregation.[3]

The Episcopal Church's canons require each diocese to "seek to resolve conflict by promoting healing, repentance, forgiveness, restitution, justice, amendment of life, and reconciliation among all involved or affected."[4]

Primary Victims

The needs of primary victims and their families vary. Each person is unique, and all efforts to support victims must be tailored to best meet that person's needs. Most importantly, the victim's perception of their needs must be honored even when those offering help view these needs differently. Help and support can be offered; its acceptance should not be coerced or mandated. Respecting the dignity of primary victims means respecting their choices. For example, many victims reporting misconduct could benefit from a professional

---

2. Title IV.8.1.

3. For further explanation on mitigating harm and weighing risks, see chapter 4.

4. Title IV.1.

supportive relationship with a therapist. However, if a victim does not perceive the need for counseling, it is inappropriate to tell a victim that he or she needs counseling. What could be said is, "Others who have been in similar situations have found working with a therapist helpful. You might want to consider this. The church (and/or bishop) wants to support you. If in the weeks or months to come you decide that counseling would be helpful to you, please let us know. We will work to make a certain number of sessions available to you." This is an approach that honors a person whose dignity and respect has been dishonored by virtue of the misconduct.[5]

Church authorities may encounter primary victims in various stages of healing from misconduct. Some will have done considerable work to move toward wholeness and will clearly articulate what they need from the church. Others will be emotionally raw and may be telling their story of victimization for the first time. It is essential to listen to all victims and not presume to know what they need. For some, just telling church authorities about their victimization significantly contributes toward their healing. As one woman said, "The hands that held out the consecrated bread to me each week were the same hands that violated me when I was a young woman. I've worked with my therapist for years, and coming here to tell the bishop how this violation stole my trust in myself and God has helped me to move forward in a way that therapy alone could not."

In general (remember everyone is unique) primary victims are best supported when they are believed as they disclose misconduct. There will be a time for questions and investigations, but in this moment, it is most helpful for the church authority to listen and receive what the victim is offering as if all of it were true.[6] This is not the time to determine the veracity of the victim's story. Victims can be thanked for bringing this information to the attention of the

---

5. This approach is referred to as "client defined advocacy." For a resource that explains the need for and how to provide assistance in this paradigm, see *Domestic Violence Advocacy: Complex Lives/Difficult Choices, 2nd Edition,* by J. Davies and E. Lyon, (Los Angeles/London/New Delhi/Singapore/Washington, DC: Sage Publications, 2014).

6. It is wise not to *affirm* that everything the victim asserts is true. The victim should be told that the church takes these concerns seriously and that there is a process to determine how to address these concerns.

church. In receiving what the victim has shared, it is important not to promise to keep the information secret. It is also important not to promise or guarantee what the outcome from reporting this information will be. You may not have control over the ultimate outcome. If you make a promise that is not fulfilled, then the church has again betrayed the victim's trust.

One aspect of pastoral care for victims is supporting them in their individual healing processes. Generally, victims report misconduct to church authorities because it is necessary as part of their healing process and to prevent others from being harmed. You can ask a victim what would promote his or her healing. Arrange to provide a set number of counseling sessions if this would be helpful to the victim. (See above regarding offering counseling services.)

You can also ask a victim if he or she has a pastor. If the alleged wrongdoer is the victim's parish priest or a key leader who the priest supports, the victim may not currently have a pastor. If the victim would find it helpful, it may be possible to identify a priest from another congregation who could serve as a temporary pastor. In seeking a priest to serve in this capacity, it is most appropriate to contact a prospective pastor and indicate that the pastoral relationship with the victim's parish priest has deteriorated. Generally, it is not appropriate to share any of the victim's story.

Some victims are concerned about the impact this will have on their family. It is advisable to ask what would be helpful to family members. Generally, it is prudent to defer to the victim as to whether or not family members will receive information about or be involved in the disciplinary process. Typically, family members benefit from much of the same support as a victim.

Giving victims general information about canonical and any other disciplinary processes supports them. This might include an oral overview and then referring to printed materials. It should also include an ongoing invitation to answer any questions as they arise. Victims also benefit from having specific information about the response process in their situation. Share what the next steps in the process will be. Inform victims of an ongoing commitment to keep them informed. Victims should be informed of progress in any investigative/disciplinary process *before* members of the congregation.

It is a best practice to tell victims as early as possible that there will likely be some details that cannot be shared with them. A bishop's work with a cleric may include pastoral concerns that should be kept confidential, even in light of misconduct. Matters that might appropriately be kept confidential include: the fact that a bishop directs a cleric to undergo a medical or psychological evaluation, and the results of such evaluation; personal issues and dynamics within the cleric's family; and personal feelings and views of the bishop or bishop's staff regarding the cleric, whether those impressions are positive or negative.

As the process moves forward, explore what will help a victim be and feel as safe as possible. Often victims are concerned about a cleric's response when he or she learns that their behavior has been reported to church authorities. Provide assurance that the victim will receive prior notification of when the cleric will be informed of the allegations. It is also helpful for victims to know that the cleric will be directed not to contact the victim or discuss the matter with anyone in the congregation, if in fact this is how the bishop will instruct the cleric. For further discussion as to why such direction is helpful, see below.

Victims benefit from receiving honest information about challenges they will likely face in the congregation. Explain that church authorities will not disclose the identity of a victim or complainant (unless a victim wants his or her identity disclosed), but based on the facts, members of the congregation may be able to determine their identity. Acknowledge that typically members of a congregation will initially blame a victim for misconduct because it is so hard for members to recognize that a trusted leader may have betrayed them. Often victims will raise this fear. They intuitively know that members will be unhappy that there will be disruption in the parish because the victim spoke his or her truth.

Victims deserve to know if the matter they reported will be (or has been) reported to secular authorities. If the nature of the alleged wrongdoing involves the abuse or neglect of children, elders, or adults dependent on others for care, state law may require a report to secular authorities. In some instances, it can be helpful to victims to be invited to make the report to secular authorities along with the church representative. Even if the victim does not want a report to be made, if the law requires such a report, a report should still be made. For a fuller discussion of mandated reporting laws, see chapter 3.

Almost all victims of clergy abuse benefit from repeated reminders that a cleric is always responsible for maintaining appropriate boundaries in a ministerial relationship. Victims will often blame themselves for what transpired. In some instances, victims will have more personal power than the cleric in terms of income, education, status, and community connections both in and beyond the church. However, on an institutional level, the cleric always has more power than those they minister to by virtue of their position in the church.

In some instances, people who are victimized as adults place greater blame on themselves than those who were victimized as children. All victims deserve to be told that they are not at fault for a cleric's abuse of power and failure to maintain appropriate boundaries in a ministerial relationship. As victims heal, many explore aspects of their personality and life circumstances that may have made them vulnerable to the abuse. Being vulnerable to abuse does not cause abuse. It can be harmful for church authorities to invite victims to explore their vulnerability because victims may hear this as being blamed for the abuse. Generally, it is most helpful to allow victims to work with skilled therapists who can explore these issues when victims are ready to look at such issues. For some, this degree of healing takes years of hard work.

The Episcopal Church's canons require a bishop to offer an advisor to a complainant or an injured person (as so designated by the bishop). An advisor is knowledgeable about the canonical disciplinary process and can provide "support, assistance, consultation, and advice" regarding the process. An advisor can serve as a companion and confidential sounding board. In addition, an advisor can be present with the complainant during many phases of the canonical disciplinary process and in some instances can be present in place of the complainant. Complainants do not need to accept or avail themselves of the assistance of an advisor offered by the bishop.[7]

---

7. Canon IV.19.10.

FOR OFFENDERS OR ALLEGED OFFENDERS

It is important to remember that those who offend are wounded themselves. On some level there is brokenness in their relationship with God and others. It is this brokenness that led to decisions and behaviors that wounded others.

There is a wide range of reasons why clergy engage in misconduct. Clergy who engage in misconduct can be thought of as falling on a continuum that runs from being naïve (unaware of appropriate boundaries and power dynamics in ministerial relationships) to being predatory (aware of boundaries and power dynamics, and knowingly exploiting them to meet personal needs at the expense of others). With increased scrutiny and background checks in the ordination process, there are fewer predators finding their way into ordained ministry in the Episcopal Church, yet there are still some. Generally, an offender who is predatory will respond with little outward emotion because he or she is so well defended. Often there is more than one primary victim, although only one victim may have contacted church authorities thus far. A predator may have great difficulty amending his or her life and behaviors.

Clergy who are naïve may have difficulty comprehending what was wrong with their behavior. Sometimes these clerics have a blind spot when it comes to boundaries in certain settings, but understand and abide by appropriate boundaries in other settings. Some clergy who are naïve may be highly motivated to learn and are able to amend their lives; some just cannot understand why their behaviors pose any problem and have great difficulty correcting their behavior.

The majority of clergy who offend fall somewhere between being naïve and predatory. Generally, this broad group of clergy lack awareness of how their behaviors impact others. When confronted with the harm they have caused, some will respond by showing little regard for the other's injuries and focus only on why their behavior was justified. Other clerics, who realize the harm their behavior caused, may be deeply pained. Those who recognize and are remorseful for the pain they caused are more able to take responsibility for the impact of their behavior and amend their lives than those who continue to justify their actions.

When allegations of clergy misconduct are raised, the bishop must provide an appropriate pastoral response to all impacted. This involves caring for the cleric in a way that prevents further harm from occurring while the disciplinary process unfolds. While clergy can benefit from many of the same supports as primary victims, there are different considerations and options available to judicatories. In short, judicatories have greater authority over clergy than lay offenders and victims.

The Episcopal Church disciplinary canons give bishops authority to impose administrative leave, restrict a cleric's ministry, or instruct a cleric to take or refrain from certain actions. Bishops do not have this authority over lay complainants or offenders.[8]

Utmost care is needed to inform alleged offenders of allegations regarding misconduct. As hard as it is for primary victims to come forward to report abuse to church authorities, at least they have chosen *when* to tell church authorities. Offenders have not chosen when, or if, their wrongdoings will be revealed. Knowledge that church authorities have information about a cleric's wrongdoings (or alleged wrongdoings) can throw the cleric into sudden crisis.

All situations and people can be redeemed through Christ. Some lose sight of this when confronted with allegations of misconduct and may consider suicide. Before informing any cleric of allegations of misconduct, it is prudent to consider whether this is a possibility and, when indicated, plan for immediate and appropriate support for the cleric.[9] Such support can include having a psychologist available on site for the cleric to meet with immediately after learning of the allegations. A psychologist will ascertain whether the cleric has plans for upcoming days and hours; if someone is making plans for the future, they aren't likely planning to harm themselves. In addition, a psychologist will listen to discern other issues the cleric may be experiencing.

---

8. Title IV.7.

9. In most cases, this consideration can be quickly dismissed. However, in those few cases where this is a risk, care must be taken to speak the truth and prevent self-harm.

Asking a cleric if he or she is considering harming him or herself can be a hard conversation to initiate, and yet it can be lifesaving. Sadly, in some situations no matter how much care is taken and support offered, a cleric will take his or her life. Not only is this a tragedy for the cleric and all those who love and care for him or her, it can leave questions about the misconduct unresolved. Unresolved questions and self-imposed guilt for suicide can make it even more challenging for primary victims and congregations to move forward.

Generally, allegations of clergy misconduct initiate a judicatory response. How that response is initiated and carried out impacts the degree of care and support clergy (and lay offenders) receive in the process. In general (remember everyone is unique), clergy and others who offend (or are alleged to have offended) will benefit by being informed of the initial meeting to discuss the matter as close to the time of the meeting as possible so that the cleric does not spend any more time than necessary anticipating the conversation. Offenders can be invited to bring a support person with them to this meeting. It is best if this support person is not a member of the congregation in which the misconduct is alleged to have occurred.

Providing clergy with information about the disciplinary process helps them know what they might expect and can reduce anxiety. This could include an oral overview and then reference to printed materials. It is helpful to explain the immediate next steps in the process and extend an invitation to answer any questions about the process as they arise.

> It is beneficial to educate all clergy about canonical disciplinary process. Informed clergy can provide support to those facing allegations.

In addition, offer as full an explanation of the allegations as possible. At this stage it may be wise to omit information that discloses the identity of the victim or complainant. Allow the cleric to ask questions and respond to the allegations. In the initial conversation to inform the cleric of the allegations, it is best to refrain from making any determination of facts or from sharing impressions of the facts at this point in the process. This is generally a preliminary conversation.

Explore whether the cleric has a pastor. Although a bishop is the pastor to all clergy of the diocese, when a disciplinary action begins, the bishop has an active role in that process. This can preclude the bishop from being able to serve as the cleric's pastor during this time. Some clergy find it helpful to identify someone who can appropriately serve as a pastor to the cleric and perhaps the cleric's family. A cleric can refuse such support. In addition, it is beneficial to help clergy identify other sources of support. Valuable sources of support can be a spiritual director, therapist, coach, mentor, trusted clergy colleague, or close friend. For clergy lacking these sources of support, exploring how some of these connections might be made is helpful.

Inquire about the welfare of family members and how they will be impacted by the allegations of misconduct. Offering to provide counseling or a pastor for family members may be appropriate.

Tell the cleric who will be informed of the pending allegations and when such notification will occur. It is preferable for a judicatory leader to inform the congregation of allegations and not rely on the cleric to disseminate such information. (See chapter 6 for a fuller discussion on methods to disclose such information to congregations.) Clerics should also be informed if the matter will be (or has been) reported to secular authorities, as required by law, i.e., if the nature of the alleged wrongdoing involves the abuse or neglect of children, elders, or adults dependent on others.

It is advisable for judicatories to specifically explore, instruct, or direct a cleric to observe clear boundaries as the process proceeds. For example, if the allegations pertain to misuse of discretionary funds, it is in everyone's best interest for the cleric to refrain from accessing the funds for the time being. In essence, this provides a "time out" while decisions can be made as to how best to move forward. As previously noted, this can be a time of heightened anxiety for clergy. No one makes his or her best decisions in the midst of high anxiety; helping to set clear boundaries for the immediate future is not only helpful to congregations, but also to clergy. This reduces the likelihood that a cleric will make poor choices, which could lead to further misconduct and/or allegations of misconduct.

The Episcopal Church's canons require a bishop to offer an advisor to a cleric charged with an offense. The name and contact information of the advisor can be provided at the same time the cleric is initially notified that allegations are pending.[10]

• • •

The Episcopal Church's canons grant bishops authority to issue a pastoral direction to any member of the clergy canonically resident, licensed, or actually resident in their diocese at any the time. Allegations of misconduct do not have to be pending.[11]

• • •

The Episcopal Church's canons grant bishops authority to restrict ministry or impose administrative leave only when a bishop determines that a cleric may have committed an offense, or that the good order, welfare, or safety of the church or persons are threatened. Administrative leave is a restriction on *all* aspects of ministry while a restriction on ministry applies to only certain aspects of ministry. If either is imposed, the cleric can seek review of the bishop's action.[12]

The care and support of primary victims, complainants, offenders, and alleged offenders is essential. While some of this support is required by the Episcopal Church's canons, there is much that can be offered beyond what is required. All care and support offered to both victims and offenders should treat them with dignity and

---

10. Title IV.19.10 contains specific provisions regarding advisors. In many cases, the canons do not require that an advisor be offered to a cleric when a cleric initially learns of allegations. However, some clergy find it helpful to have the advisor present when they are first informed of the specifics of the allegations. Understandably, clergy are usually very anxious during these conversations, and anxiety impedes the ability to process information. Advisors can help offenders process the information and compose questions.

11. Title IV.7 addresses pastoral directions. When allegations of misconduct are pending, a pastoral direction can help clergy refrain from taking actions that could make matters worse. The following conditions could be included in a pastoral direction: refrain from initiating contact or engaging in any communication with the primary victim; refrain from discussing the fact of or nature of the allegations with any members of the congregation; use sources of support offered by the bishop/diocese such as counseling or medical/psychological evaluation. It is best to fully explain all provisions of a pastoral direction to a cleric, because any violation of a pastoral direction can result in new allegations in a disciplinary process.

12. See Title IV.7.

respect. They are in the midst of very difficult circumstances. Such care and support may include encouragement to recognize the need to amend one's life and take responsibility for any harm caused to oneself or others.

The care and support of these individuals happens simultaneously with the care and support of parish leaders and all members of the congregation. These multiple parallel processes of care and support intersect at key moments, requiring judicatories to balance the needs of all impacted by misconduct. Appendix I contains a checklist that can be used to help ensure all aspects of care and support for victims and offenders are considered.

12

Integration

HEALING AND CLOSURE

There will come a time when most members and the congregation as a whole will integrate the experience of betrayal in their lives and return their focus to engaging in God's mission, here and now. This integration can occur only after members face misconduct, know all the facts that can be disclosed, allow themselves to fully experience the betrayal, accept and honor that others respond differently, recognize and acknowledge their own role in any breaches in relationships among members, forgive themselves and other members, and recreate or build healthy new relationships within the congregation. Some members will not be able to complete this work for a variety of reasons. It is essential that the congregation hold these members in community as the congregation brings closure to the active work of healing from betrayal.

Integration of betrayal does not mean that the members and the congregation will never again focus on the misconduct. There will be events in the life of the congregation and lives of its members that bring past misconduct to the forefront. These are opportunities to further reflect on how they have been formed and recreated in the wake of misconduct—all who engage in this work and face misconduct in their congregations are different than they were before the misconduct, including the congregation as a whole.[1] Healing and

---

1. This ongoing work can be triggered by a seemingly unrelated event and is often spoken of as healing work that is akin to peeling the layers of an onion. As new layers are opened, there is deeper healing and restoration possible.

restoring trust are ongoing processes. What is brought to closure is the degree of focus, time, and energy intentionally directed toward processes to respond to the misconduct.

As humans we like to have a certain degree of order and control in our lives. When faced with difficult situations, we want to know, "How long will it take to deal with this?" and "When can we get on with our lives?" When it comes to misconduct in a congregation, the restoration continues, to some degree, indefinitely. This is difficult to accept. Some vestries will want to schedule an event to declare that healing has been completed even as they are scheduling the initial disclosure meetings. It's as if getting this on the calendar will make it true—that we all will be healed and restored by a specified date. It's simply not that easy, and it's impossible to predict how long a congregation will need to focus its time and energy on response work before members integrate the experience of betrayal.

There will come a time when parish leaders can declare that it is time to refocus efforts away from the work of responding to misconduct. This refocusing should not cut off efforts to continue to heal, integrate, and be transformed in the wake of misconduct. Declaring that the work of healing is complete can cause harm. Those members still struggling with difficult responses to misconduct may feel shame or alienation from the congregation if they are not "healed" as others seem to be. Any communication or event, including liturgical events, intended to mark the shift in focus from responding to misconduct to engaging God's mission beyond the congregation, needs to make clear that this marks a shift in focus—not the end of the work.

Integration of misconduct, both individually and corporately, requires members to know the facts and understand the impact this betrayal has had on them and the congregation. There can be no secret keeping or denying the hurt. Rather, members must have faced the facts and experienced their feelings within a framework that provides support and normalizes feelings many people find challenging to experience, such as anger, sadness, and loss. Members integrate this experience of betrayal with all their other life experiences. Having faced this, members are freed from spending time and energy suppressing feelings and keeping secrets.

A key element in integration is an understanding and acceptance of the differences in members' experience of and reactions to misconduct. Longtime friends who had been joined at the hip may now need to reestablish aspects of their relationship (and perhaps forgive themselves and each other) when they initially could not support each other because of the differences in how they reacted to misconduct. Sometimes these differences are due, in part, to the leadership responsibilities of one of the members.

In efforts to move the congregation forward, ordained and lay leadership need to take care not to demonize or dismiss those who are not ready to move forward or appear "stuck" in their reactions to misconduct. This may indicate a need for additional support for some individual members, perhaps one-to-one conversations with a pastor, spiritual director, or clinician. It requires the acceptance that each member is doing the best he or she can.

In the midst of the pain of betrayal, members need to recognize their own part in causing harm to others and relationships. This is hard work. Often this work cannot begin until members have first worked through how they were harmed by others. For some, it is only after that initial work that they can ask, "What role did I play in this?" They may have ignored warning signs, not believed members who initially raised concerns, or acted in ways that were divisive to the congregation or relationships among members—perhaps out of anger or as a way of protecting themselves from feeling the full impact of misconduct. It is natural, and perhaps an evolutionary defense mechanism, to first focus on our own well-being when facing misconduct, before we can turn our attention to how we have harmed others.

At some point, members will need to offer and seek forgiveness to fully integrate the experience of misconduct. Forgiveness is not about glossing over what happened or condoning or excusing unacceptable, hurtful behavior. It is about seeking peace after having honestly and fully faced a situation by making a conscious decision to let go of resentment and anger, even in the face of harm done by others. The decision to seek inner peace can be made even when the person who harmed you has not taken responsibility for their actions. In other words, they may not deserve your forgiveness, but you offer it anyway.

True forgiveness and peace happens by making the conscious decision to forgive others, accompanied by the gift of grace. To forgive is a conscious decision; when combined with grace, it is a relief and a release. If members have protected themselves from fully experiencing the betrayal, perhaps by holding on to anger and blame directed at the offender or others, it can be hard to forgive. It can become a pattern—a coping mechanism. The process of responding to misconduct needs to create a safe environment so members can "try on" another way of being and discontinue old patterns.

In addition to forgiving others, members need to take responsibility for the harm they caused and seek forgiveness by offering an apology. This requires recognizing the impact of their behavior on others and taking responsibility for that impact—even if no harm was intended. To apologize for the harm inflicted on another requires taking responsibility for that harm—the impact of one's behavior or words. When it comes to apologies and seeking forgiveness, it doesn't matter if the harm was intended or not. Apologizing for hurting someone by saying, "Sorry, I really had only good intentions and didn't mean to hurt you," can have the effect of minimizing the other's harm and diminishing the responsibility accepted for that harm. If you get run over by a car, it causes bodily harm. The bodily harm is the same whether the driver intended to run you over or not.

Finally, members must be able to forgive themselves for the harm they caused others, even if the others are not offering forgiveness. Seeking forgiveness from oneself can be hard. Continuing to live in guilt and self-blame is not what God intended for any of us. Our sins have already been redeemed through Christ. Holding onto guilt over past transgressions values a human standard of justice above God's. "So if anyone is in Christ, there is a new creation: everything old has passed away; see, everything has become new!"[2] Holding onto guilt is preventing the old from passing away and the new from coming into being. As members work to accept that others did the best that they could in these difficult circumstances, members need to apply this to themselves. Through our willingness to forgive ourselves, we may be able to see patterns in our own behavior previously

---

2. 2 Corinthians 5:17.

unseen—self-forgiveness is not only a release from guilt, it can help us pierce through denial.

Forgiveness is an essential step before alienated members can recreate or build healthy trusting relationships with each other. Individual members and the community are transformed by having experienced misconduct and intentionally engaged in a healing process. Relationships among members will be different. As trust is restored within the congregation, relationships among members are recreated—they may have new boundaries and different levels of intimacy than before the misconduct.

For members to forgive themselves and others, and recreate healthy relationships, they need to feel safe and not live in fear of future misconduct in their church. An essential component of closure is ensuring that the risk of future misconduct is reduced to the greatest extent possible. This requires that members know what happened (or what is alleged to have happened) and understand power, vulnerability, and boundaries in ministerial relationships. This understanding can help deepen members' appreciation of how the misconduct occurred, as well as ways to reduce the risk of reoccurrence. Reducing future risks may require new policies and practices. New policies should be drafted to be brief (so members will read them), clear (so members will understand them), and then distributed on a regular basis and posted in accessible areas of the congregation's meeting spaces. Misconduct in a congregation affects all members. The prevention of misconduct and rebuilding of a healthy community of faith is the responsibility of all members, not just those in leadership.

As members within a congregation begin to restore trust, the intentional focus on the work of healing from misconduct can begin to shift to engaging God's mission beyond the congregation and walls of the church. Even after this shift of focus occurs, further healing can take place as events in the lives of members and the congregation may again bring misconduct to the forefront. And when this happens, these individuals and communities are better equipped to further integrate additional insights, by having intentionally focused on the work of restoring trust in the wake of misconduct. This challenge of restoring wholeness in our relationships with one another and with God is our highest calling as Christians.

Prayer for Reconciliation with Others[3]

Lord, I have not always been the best sign of your love.
I've hurt others in my church and I've hurt you.

Help me to forgive myself.
Help me to return to you.

I haven't remembered that
    everything I am and have
    is a gift from you.
I'm praying to you.
Forgive me.

I will do my best to be a new person,
A better person,
Today and every day.

Give me strength to say I'm sorry to those I have hurt.
Help us to start fresh.

---

3. *Call On Me: A Prayer Book for Young People* by Jenifer C. Gamber and Sharon Ely Pearson (New York: Morehouse Publishing, 2012), 93. Adapted and used with permission.

APPENDIX A

❦

Weighing the Risks

STEPS AND CHART

The chart below (referred to in chapter 4) can be used in the decision-making process by weighing the risks of acting or not acting.

DECISION-MAKING PROCESS: WEIGHING THE RISKS OF ACTING AND NOT ACTING	
STEP 1: Choose a specific action	
STEP 2: List risks of taking action	**STEP 3: List ways to reduce or eliminate risks identified in Step 2**
STEP 4: List risks of *not* taking action	**STEP 5: List ways to reduce or eliminate risks identified in Step 4**
STEP 6: Decision	

APPENDIX B

ᏝᎮᏝ

Disclosure Statement

WORKSHEET

This worksheet can be used to determine the content of what will be disclosed and what is appropriately held in confidence as discussed in chapter 5.

1. Start with the truth.

List all the key facts that you are aware of regarding the incidents of misconduct, including who, what, when, and where.

2. Balance the need for transparency with confidentially.

In consultation with the bishop, consider whether there is pastorally sensitive or personal information about the offender, victims(s), their families, or the person who reported misconduct that should appropriately remain confidential. List those considerations.

3. Use information from public records if possible.

Are there any public documents? If so, what are they? What information is contained in those documents?

4. Avoid disclosing the identity of primary victim(s).

Review the statement to be sure that the name, identifying characteristics, and pronouns indicating gender are removed that could reveal the victim's identity. (Skip this if the victim has made an informed decision to disclose his or her identify.)

5. Identify whether victims are minors or adults in cases involving sexual misconduct.

6. Be brief.

Remove all facts that are non-essential. Details about the disciplinary process can be provided in response to questions.

7. Have legal counsel review the content of the statement.

This is done *before* the statement is shared with anyone.

APPENDIX C

Sample Disclosure Statements for Congregations

Bishop's statement regarding misconduct by an ordained leader in a parish:

This past week I learned that Rev. Z had an inappropriate relationship outside of his marriage with an adult woman who received pastoral care from Rev. Z. This behavior on the part of any priest is not acceptable. As a result, I met with Rev. Z on Wednesday morning. I informed him of the seriousness of this matter and Rev. Z resigned as priest of this parish at that meeting.

This week I met with your wardens and officers to begin the work of looking forward to the future, as well as healing from this loss. The Rev. Y will be performing services at your church through [date].

Please know that my staff is working to provide care and support to all those affected by this situation. I am holding this parish, Rev. Z and Y, and all other individuals affected by this situation in my prayers.

Bishop's statement regarding misconduct by an ordained leader in a parish:

It has come to my attention that the Rev. Z, your interim rector, violated safe church protocols as set in place by our diocese. The violations I am aware of do not involve children or minors.

I asked for and have received Rev. Z's resignation as interim rector of St. B's.

I and [name of judicatory staff member] will meet again with the leadership of St. B's on Tuesday evening and then return on Thursday to meet with the staff to assist in determining how best to move forward at this time.

Rector and wardens' statement regarding allegations of sexual abuse of minor by lay member/leader:

It is our responsibility to advise parish members that allegations of sexual misconduct have been received against Y, a member of our church. These allegations stem from a time about ten years ago and involve a person who was a minor at that time. Y denies these allegations. These allegations have been reported to the appropriate civil authorities.

APPENDIX D

ⓔⓣⓣⓣⓞ

Sample Statements
for the Press

From a bishop regarding allegations of sexual abuse of a minor by an ordained leader:

On [date], Bishop X, bishop of the Diocese of ABC, placed the Reverend Z on Administrative Leave after receiving allegations that he engaged in sexual contact with a minor. The bishop has notified the appropriate civil authorities. Care and support has been and will continue to be made available to all individuals affected and the congregation of St. B's, where Father Z was serving.

From a bishop in response to litigation filed against a parish and/or diocese for failing to protect children:

In [month and year], a bishop of the Episcopal Church learned for the first time of allegations that a minor had been sexually abused at [name of church] years earlier. In response, the bishop immediately reported this abuse to secular authorities as required by state law and the policies of the Episcopal Church. In addition, the bishop started a series of open discussions among the members of the parish to identify any other victims and to begin a transparent healing process in the community.

A disciplinary proceeding, in accordance with the canons (laws) of the Episcopal Church, would have commenced against Z, the priest of the parish at the time of the alleged abuse. This disciplinary action would have focused on Z's failure to report suspected abuse as required by state law and our church policies. Z has since renounced his orders as a priest in the Episcopal Church. This means Z is no longer a priest in the Episcopal Church and any church disciplinary proceedings would have no effect.

For many years the Episcopal Church has implemented strong policies to prevent any abuse of minors and to respond quickly and effectively to allegations of abuse. All those impacted by child sexual abuse remain in our prayers.

APPENDIX E

ᏮᎢᎢᎯᎮ

Disclosure Meeting

SAMPLE INVITATIONS FOR MEMBERS

As discussed in chapter 6, invitations to disclosure meetings should contain enough information so members know what the meeting is about, but not disclose information that hasn't already been shared. Below are sample invitations that have been used in a variety of situations.

Invitation issued by lay leaders and the bishop in response to misconduct by an ordained leader:

Your wardens, vestry, and Bishop X invite all adult members of St. B's to attend an important meeting in the life of our congregation on [date and time] at St. B's parish hall. Bishop X has information to share regarding the leadership of our parish and the challenges we are facing.

This will be a time for us to gather together, understand these challenges, and explore ways to minister to each other as we move forward. Please make every effort to attend.

Invitation issued by a bishop in response to misconduct by an ordained leader:

On [date] I will be at your church, along with [name of other facilitator and title], to meet with members of the parish and respond to questions that you may have regarding Rev. A's recent arrest. I urge you to attend this meeting so that I might have the opportunity to hear and respond to your questions directly. Your wardens and vestry will decide and notify you of the time of this meeting.

Please know that your diocesan staff and I are working to provide care and support to all those affected by this situation, including Rev. A.

Invitation issued by ordained leader after arrest of a lay leader:

As you may have learned through the press, a member of our church who has participated in various activities, ministries, and programs of St. B's was arrested by the [town] police at the end of last week and charged with possession of internet child pornography.

This type of news raises many questions and concerns. In light of this, we have asked [judicatory consultant/pastoral response coordinator] to be among us for an open meeting in our church on Thursday evening, [date] at 7:30 p.m. [Name of consultant/judicatory staff] has worked with a number of other parishes in our diocese that have encountered similar situations. This is a meeting for all adult and teenage members of our parish. We will have an opportunity to freely and safely discuss concerns and issues, and to respond to questions.

Though this is very short notice, we want to provide this initial opportunity for conversation as soon as possible.

Please pray for all those impacted by this situation.

Invitation issued by parish clergy and wardens regarding allegations of sexual abuse of a minor by lay leader:

It is our responsibility to advise parish members that allegations of misconduct have been received against a member and leader of St. B's.

We are convening a meeting for members of St. B's on [date and time] so we, together with [name of judicatory staff member], can have an opportunity to talk about the effect of these allegations, and how to live and move forward together as a Christian community.

In the days ahead, please avoid the temptations of speculation and gossip, and do keep all those concerned and our parish in your prayers.

Invitation issued by parish clergy and lay leaders in response to misconduct by a lay leader:

We are writing to invite you to a meeting for members of St. B's parish on Monday, [date] at 7:00 p.m.

An incident at our parish has become the focus of legal proceedings; some members of our parish are aware of this, others are not. The parish is not a party in the legal proceedings.

The purpose of the meeting is to learn how we, as a community of faith, can respond to the numerous individuals affected and the parish community. A diocesan staff member and a consultant will be with us to lead our discussion.

In the meantime, please refrain from gossip and speculation. If you have questions or concerns, please speak with us (the undersigned wardens and clergy). We ask your prayers for all members of our congregation.

APPENDIX F

〇ᵐᵐᵐᵐ〇

Disclosure Meeting

GATHERING QUESTIONS
AND CONCERNS FORM

This form is a tool to assist facilitators in organizing questions asked by congregation members during a disclosure meeting. Facilitators are invited to modify this form to best meet their needs. The categories are those that commonly arise.

Categories of Questions or Topics	Questions or Topics of Concern as Expressed by Members	Check Off (When Response Has Been Provided)
Disclosure statement clarification: Who knew what, when?		
Disciplinary process as set out by canon		
Involvement of secular authorities (child protective services, local or state police, etc.)		

Continued

Categories of Questions or Topics	Questions or Topics of Concern as Expressed by Members	Check Off (When Response Has Been Provided)
Identity of victim(s) and/or complainant(s); may require reiteration of why identities not disclosed		
How could this happen here? Breakdown in safe church protocols, and/or focus on nature of misconduct, *i.e.*, child sex abuse, embezzlement		
How can we prevent this from happening again?		
Care for those impacted	Offender: Offender's family: Primary victim(s): Congregation:	
Day-to-day concerns going forward		
Working with the media		

APPENDIX G

Additional Statement and Invitation from Wardens

Dear brothers and sisters in Christ,

Father Z's departure from our church has raised many feelings. We shared some of these feelings when we met with Bishop X and [name of judicatory staff member] on [date]. To provide us with a supportive environment in which to further explore and share these feelings, a meeting has been arranged for [time] on Sunday, [date]. [Name of judicatory staff member] will be with us to facilitate this meeting, along with a colleague, Dr. [name of psychologist]. This team has worked with congregations wrestling with issues of loss and transition of the sort we are facing here at our church. We invite you to come spend time with us if you feel such a gathering would be helpful to you.

In the meantime, if you have any questions or need assistance with any church-related function, please feel free to contact either of us.

APPENDIX H

Disclosure Meeting

OUTLINE OF RESPONSIBILITIES

This outline is offered as a tool to assist those responding to misconduct in a congregation, for the assigning of roles and responsibilities in conducting a disclosure meeting (as discussed in chapter 6).

Before disclosure meeting:

Inviting members to attend:

> Name of lay leader responsible for this communication:
>
> Who assists lay leader with content?
>
> How and when is invitation communicated to members?

Room setup:

> What will configuration be?
>
> Who is responsible for setup?

Microphone needed?

> If so, who is responsible for setup and operation?

Supplies needed (flip chart, name tags, markers, etc.):

> Who is responsible for these supplies?

Presence of offender, primary victim(s), and/or complainant(s):

> Will any of these people be present? Who?
>
> Who is their source of support during the meeting?

Subject matter expert needed (*i.e.*, embezzlement or child sexual abuse)?

> If so, who is the expert?
>
> Who explains the design of the meeting to the expert?

Flip chart listing categories of information prepared by:

Disclosure meeting to staff and/or others immediately preceding disclosure to congregation:

Are there individuals uniquely impacted by the misconduct who should be informed in a small group before disclosure to the entire congregation?

Will staff be informed of the misconduct prior to disclosure to the congregation?

> If so, when and where will these meeting(s) be held?
>
> Who invites staff or others to attend?
>
> Who facilitates these meetings? (Ideally the same as those who will facilitate the congregational disclosure meeting.)

Overview of components of disclosure meeting:

Who does what during the meeting? Insert the name of the facilitator who will lead/present each segment.

1. Opening prayer:
2. Introductory matters:
3. Educational segment:
4. Reading of disclosure statement:
5. Gathering members' questions, comments, concerns, and then responding:

> Explains and facilitates gathering of questions:
>
> Records questions and concerns (more than one person):
>
> Responds to gathered questions:

6. Next steps:

7. Closing prayer:

After the disclosure meeting:

Is follow up needed with a victim who chose not to attend?

   If so, who does that follow up?

Is follow up needed with an offender?

   If so, who does that follow up?

Is follow up needed with any others who may have been uniquely impacted by the misconduct?

   If so, who does that follow up?

APPENDIX I

⟨ʍʍ⟩

Checklist for Care of Victims and Offenders

Each victim and offender is unique. This checklist may be used to customize care and support to address specific needs of an individual. Each item listed is discussed in chapter 11.

For victims:

☐ Receive the victim's story without judgment during the initial reporting of the alleged misconduct.

☐ Offer support in the victim's healing process. Is counseling needed? Do they currently have a pastor?

☐ Share general information about canonical or other applicable disciplinary processes.

☐ Provide as much detailed information as possible about the process as it applies to the situation.

☐ Inform victims that some details cannot be shared with them.

☐ Offer support for the victim's family. Ask what would be helpful to his or her family members.

☐ Explore what would help the victim be and feel as safe as possible.

☐ Share honest information about the likely challenges victims may face in the congregation.

☐ Explain if the matter will be (or has been) reported to secular authorities.

☐ Consider whether an advisor should be offered pursuant to the disciplinary canons of the Episcopal Church. (Title IV.19.10.)

☐ Remind victims that a cleric is always responsible for maintaining appropriate boundaries in a ministerial relationship.

For offenders or alleged offenders:[1]

☐ Consider the possibility of self-harm and reduce its likelihood.

☐ Inform the offender of the meeting regarding allegations as close to the time of the meeting as possible.

☐ Invite the offender to bring a support person to the initial meeting.

☐ Provide information about the disciplinary process.

☐ Offer as full an explanation of the allegations as possible.

☐ Allow and/or ask the offender to respond to the allegations.

☐ Identify a pastor for the offender, if so desired.

☐ Explore and identify a range of sources of support, such as spiritual director, therapist, close friend.

☐ Offer support for the offender's family. Ask what would be helpful to his or her family members.

☐ Explain if the matter will be (or has been) reported to secular authorities.

☐ Consider whether an advisor should be offered pursuant to the disciplinary canons of the Episcopal Church. (Title IV.19.10.)

☐ Specifically explore, instruct, or direct the offender to observe clear boundaries.

---

1. This checklist focuses on ordained offenders. Many of the same offerings are also appropriate for lay offenders.

☐ Consider whether a pastoral direction, restriction on ministry or administrative leave will be issued or imposed pursuant to the disciplinary canons of the Episcopal Church. (Title IV.7.) Review the terms of any such document with the cleric.

☐ Inform the offender of who will be told of the pending allegations and when such notification will occur.

INDEX